The Simplexity of Abundance
– 4 Steps to Plenty

"Knowing what Law of Attraction is is one thing. Knowing how to apply it to your life is another. What is missing for most people is the how-to on applying Law of Attraction deliberately. This book is a great resource for Law of Attraction students who want to know how-to apply Law of Attraction – and this book delivers. **The Simplexity of Abundance – 4 Steps to Plenty** *provides the reader with tools, scripts, and exercises to tap into the powerful Law of Attraction to get awesome results."*

– Michael Losier, Author <u>Law of Attraction: The Science of Attracting More of What You Want and Less of What You Don't</u>, www.LawofAttractionBook.com

"An excellent book. Ariole K. Alei's **The Simplexity of Abundance** *is a most comprehensive book on understanding prosperity principles. In addition to the* **4 Steps to Plenty**, *there are dozens of power points to help the reader set a new tone in consciousness for a life more abundant."*

– John Randolph Price, Bestselling author <u>The Angels Within Us</u> and <u>The Abundance Book</u> and Chairman of the Quartus Foundation, www.quartus.org

"If you liked <u>The Secret</u> and what it uncovered about the Law of Attraction, then you are in for a real treat with **The Simplexity of Abundance – 4 Steps to Plenty** *and its deeper exploration. Imagine <u>The Secret</u> with more substance and tools as to how you can REALLY achieve true abundance and joy in ALL aspects of your life!"*

– Jodi Smith, Arts Publicist, JLS Entertainment

*"Ariole K. Alei is a tour de force in the ever-evolving subject of Metaphysics and Spiritual realms. In **The Simplexity of Abundance – 4 Steps to Plenty** as well as her other books, she has an ability to make the unseen, seen. She truly has lived her writings and thus has the effortless ability to simplify the complex and make it accessible."*

– **Peter Williams**, Director of Photography, Ex CNN Cameraman / Producer, Co-founder www.LifeChangingTV.com

*"**The Simplexity of Abundance – 4 Steps to Plenty** is another masterpiece by author and visionary Ariole K. Alei. I was privileged to have been one of the first to read her manuscript, and I was immediately delighted by the way in which she eloquently succeeds at simplifying mental constructs which at times can appear complex by nature. As a Spiritual Life Coach I read books through the eyes of a teacher and a student. From my perspective **The Simplexity Of Abundance – 4 Steps to Plenty** clearly enriches the mind and heart of both. Like The Four Agreements, Law of Attraction and Power vs. Force, this book will become highly recommended reading for all of my clients who are committed to their evolutionary path of enlightenment."*

– **Colin Hillstrom**, Trainer, Speaker, Life Coach, Healer and Author When A Man Really Loves A Woman – Why We Must Love More And What To Do About It and Your 2nd Life – How to LIVE the LIFE You ALWAYS WANTED

*"What a pleasure it is to read this "Boundless" knowledge. **The Simplexity of Abundance – 4 Steps to Plenty** is a truly remarkable journey of mindful awareness of the inner and outer worlds around us. It reads like a warm place to come into, get settled, look around, rest your soul, and walk out renewed. Bravo!*

– **Lynn James**, Interior Designer, Feng Shui and Staging-for-Resale Consultant, Former Flight Attendant lynnlajames@hotmail.com

*"**The Simplexity of Abundance – 4 Steps to Plenty** should replace the bible!"*

– **Anonymous**

*"Thank you for writing **The Simplexity of Abundance – 4 Steps to Plenty**. My immediate thought when I read it was this: It is <u>the one</u> to keep out for those days when you are feeling misaligned. Its easy readable style and quick exercises have given me results right away. This is a book which illuminates and rejuvenates abundance principles."*

– **Donna Chesney**, Entrepreneur and former Registered Nurse

*"I enjoyed absorbing your thoughts in **The Simplexity of Abundance – 4 Steps to Plenty**. It is so true that our conditioned and domesticated self - the true habitat of the 'don't-change-anything ego' - keeps us from our higher self, defined as clear new thinking not negatively compromised by pre-(past)-conceptions. Your "Breakthrough" practice should strongly assist in understanding the 'Being' in our Human being. We ARE our inner conversation which directs our feelings. Correcting the way we speak to ourselves will result in improved results: better being → better actions → better results. We have to believe the life we want is possible; and we have to believe it's possible for us. Reading **The Simplexity of Abundance – 4 Steps to Plenty** is an exciting and treasured experience."*

– **David Hastings**, Business Owner

*"At the time I was introduced to **The Simplexity of Abundance** I was attempting to resolve a difficult personal situation. My mind was obsessed with this topic of WHAT I DIDN'T WANT. As I glanced through the **4 Steps to Plenty** I recognized that the principles and tools offered in this book would provide the "plenty" I was longing for.*

"Ariole's clear direction brought me back again and again to the principle that, to get what I want, THAT is what I had to focus on instead, and I had to ALLOW myself to have it. I discovered, to my surprise, that I actually felt huge resistance to having what I wanted. I was actually pushing away the resolution I wanted rather than bringing it closer!

"As I read further I was brought repeatedly to the NECESSITY of allowing ONLY what I wanted into my thoughts and feelings. Within an hour I was completely out of my resistance and this long-standing issue had dissolved into nothing. What had seemed complex was actually very simple. I now celebrate having what I truly want in this area of my life.

*"As I integrate these **4 Steps to Plenty** into my life, it is clear that if I know what I want, if I can picture having it, and if I can feel good contemplating having it, then I WILL HAVE IT! OF COURSE! Thank you, Ariole, for the clarity of this amazing and valuable new book."*

– **Jan Rosgen**, Artist, Art Coach and Graphic Designer

The Simplexity of Abundance

4 Steps to Plenty

The Simplexity of Abundance

4 Steps to Plenty

Ariole K. Alei

♥ HeartSong Solutions™

Vancouver, Canada

Published by HeartSong Solutions™
PO Box 647 - 2768 West Broadway
Vancouver, BC, Canada, V6K 4P4
www.veraxis.net, www.HeartSongSolutions.ca

Cover Design: Jan Rosgen (www.janrosgen.com)
Earth Logo: www.veraxis.net
Dove: Birds' Eye View – A Travel Guide to the Universe
Charts and Illustrations: Ariole K. Alei
Editorial Assistance: Colin Hillstrom, Donna Chesney, Ralph Danyluk,
Jodi Smith, Jan Rosgen, Lynn James, Samantha Lynn, Sat Jiwan, David
Hastings, Jane Alam, Peter Williams and other kind souls
Production and Printing: Lulu, Inc.

Library and Archives Canada Cataloguing in Publication

Alei, Ariole K., 1961 -
      The simplexity of abundance : 4 steps to plenty / Ariole K. Alei.

Includes bibliographical references.
ISBN 978-1-4303-2902-2

      1. Success. I. Title.

BF637.S4A386 2007   158.1   C2007-902395-9

Distribution: info@veraxis.net
               http://www.HeartSongSolutions.ca/products.html
               www.lulu.com/HeartSong

Simplexity:

Taking something *complex*

and presenting it in a way that reveals its *simplicity*.

"Simplexity: simplicity on the other side of complexity"

"[I am] a long-time student of mathematics and complexity theory. Frequent paradigm shifts have marked scientific thought through the ages - from classical laws to chaos theory and complexity theory. 'Simplexity' refers to the tendency of a simpler order to emerge from complexity.

"It means a simple, user-friendly way to address people's needs based on understanding the complexity of what [they] need and when.

"People's busy lives require simplicity. At the same time, complexity is increasing because the range of [options] is becoming so broad. In truth, [life] is simple. It shouldn't get more complicated as you delve down. I say simplify wherever possible.

"Simplexity takes nature's best and creates what is good and right and easy and beautiful."

– Rick France, Metaphysical Teacher and Entrepreneur

Contents

Acknowledgments   xii

How to Use This Book   xix

Introduction   xxiii

Where Plenty Comes From   xxvii

Is There Enough?   xxix

Four Steps to Plenty   xxxi

Step 1 - Know What You Want   1

Contrast - Opposite - Clarity!   6

'State Line'   10

'3 Chairs'   13

Doing in the Physical versus

Allowing in the Non-Physical   17

The Four Archetypes   21

Your Inner King/Queen   23

Your Inner Magician   26

Your Inner Warrior   28

Your Inner Lover   32

Your Four Archetypes as Allies in Your Desires   35

How Do We Open Ourselves to the Vertical Reality?   39

Meditate   40

Breathing Like a Sponge   41

Why Meditate?   45

Connecting More Frequently with your
Inner King/Queen and Lover   48

Take Your Focus Off of 'Doing' and 'Thinking'
and Place It On 'Visioning' and 'Loving'   50

Simply Be Aware of Both the Non-Physical
and the Physical Nature of Existence   53

Simplexity Summary So Far   56

Step 2 - Focus Your Attention Upon It   57

Value What You Want   68

Express Gratitude   71

Write 'My Attention Journal'   73

Use a Reminder Bell   76

'Zoom In, Zoom Out'   79

Create a Vision Board or Box   83

Declare Affirmations   86

Converse With My Non-Physical Self   91

Simplexity Summary So Far   *96*

Step 3 - Be Aware of How You Feel   97

The 17 Levels of Consciousness   104

Deciding   109

Get On the Merry Go Round   111

Inner Thinking, Outer Thinking   113

Doubt   117

How Do I Want to Feel Afterwards?   124

Experiential Rehearsals   128

Simplexity Summary So Far   *133*

Step 4 - Get Out of The Way   135

Letting Your Non-Physical Self In   137

Resistance   140

Psychosomatic Energetics   141

Core Transformation   145

The 12 Soul Powers   147

'The Beauty I See In You Is ...'   150

"Don't Think Too Much"   155

'Stop' Button   159

'Shred It'   161

Know It Will Come   167

Adjusting Your Thermostat   171

Let Go (Non-Attachment to the Outcome)   175

'Moving Hands'   181

Turn It Over To Gestation   185

Accept What Is, En-Joy, and Be Patient   193

Practice Smiling   195

Self Acceptance   201

Simplexity Summary So Far   *208*

Becoming a Master Creator   **211**

Understanding   213

Tools   217

Practice   219

Consistent and Reliable Results   222

The Amazing Alchemy of Transformation   225

Simplexity Summary So Far   *229*

Celebrating Your Successes   **231**

Creation Log   235

Yes! Yes! Yes!   237

My List of Ways To Celebrate   239

Milestones   241

Creating a Ceremony of Gratitude   243

Simplexity Summary So Far   246

Ethical Abundance   249

Creating with Consciousness   251

Your Ecological Footprint   253

Social Awareness   256

Questions and Responses   259

Afterword   261

Recommended Reading / Bibliography   263

About the Author   265

Acknowledgments

I wish to thank Life for filling me with experiences from which I have so tremendously learned; Colin for his incredible partnership on this journey; my parents, siblings and extended family for their desire to share Life in such a remarkable way with me; the friends who have been my companions along this path; the AT Group, **HeartSong** Members and *Veraxis* Clients who have given me such amazing opportunities to learn and to refine my inquiry into the Great Mystery; the natural gifts with which I've been endowed; and of course, you, for reading these words and valuing my life work.

Thank You.

How to Use This Book

What you hold in your hands is a treasure map. Within it lie great riches which become yours as you lay claim to them. You do this through Understanding and Practice.

I suggest that you read the entire book through once to gain a sense of its scope. This canopy of context will infuse even greater power into your Understanding and Tools as you will have a sense of them in relation to the 'whole'.

I recommend that you give yourself permission to mark up your copy of this book. You may wish to create a 'code'. Here is an example ...

    V - validates your existing Understanding

    N - a new idea to contemplate and explore

    $\sqrt{}$ - a Tool that you feel somewhat drawn to Practice

    $\sqrt{}\sqrt{}$ - a Tool that inspires and energizes you to Practice

You will find the following symbol throughout this book. It denotes Exercises for you to explore ...

Once you've read the book through and have marked it with your 'code' ... reflect on the insights you have gained and how reading it has benefited you.

Then ...

- Take time re-reading and reflecting on the **N** new ideas

- Re-read the **V** validations whenever you notice yourself encountering doubt as to your worthiness to claim the richness in life that you desire

- Practice the √√ Tools that particularly excite you

- Practice the √ Tools as well, noticing if your lesser enthusiasm for them is a matter of style or of resistance within you. If it is the latter, you will most definitely want to work with your √√ Tools to dissolve that resistance. For it is as and when we are no longer in resistance - taking our 'feet off the brakes' - that we allow and receive that which we truly desire.

Enjoy this book! The treasures within it have the benevolent power to free you from your conditioned experience of lack into your eternal experience of plenty.

Everyone has access to this treasure. All of our limitations, ultimately, are within.

Here's to your life of joy, freedom and ease ... *in this moment ... now!*

We are already abundant
- an 'aha' which we all realize in the process of
'becoming' abundant. In fact it is the
remembering of this truth
which opens the sacred door
to our ultimate plenty.

Introduction

The ability to create that which we truly desire is surprisingly simple. So simple that most of us oversee it and instead spend our precious lives working hard to create more of what we *don't* want. In other words - struggle which generates more struggle.

How to create precisely what we want *with ease - and consistency* has been private knowledge held by a rare few - those born or invited into lineages of this esoteric wisdom.

This powerful wisdom is recently coming into mainstream access through a wide variety of teachings, among them the books of Napoleon Hill, John Randolph Price, Abraham-Hicks, Michael Losier, T. Harv Eker and many others. Plus the DVD "The Secret" has inspired so many people around the world with the promise of abundance.

We are already abundant - an 'aha' which we all realize in the process of 'becoming' abundant. In fact it is the remembering of this truth which opens the sacred door to our ultimate plenty.

Abundance exists in all things - and therefore it exists in all areas of our life. Some think of abundance as being monetary. It is. And it is so much more. *True* abundance - living a truly abundant life - is living in *flow* in each and *every* facet of our life. True abundance is Life Balance, being tapped in to an infinite stream of goodness.

Abundance therefore can be abundance - plenty, *flow* – in

- Health
- Relationship
- Mental clarity
- Open-heartedness
- Business / career
- Volunteering
- Personal fulfillment
- Finances
- And so much more …

In this simple book - <u>The Simplexity of Abundance</u> - we will explore the four key steps to attracting and receiving - in other words, creating - anything you desire. *Anything.*

With mastery - which arises naturally with patience and practice - you, too, can discover the indescribable relief and excitement of knowing how to consistently create the plenty that you seek in life.

No one is exempt from this. We are all equally capable of having plenty - of experiencing 'plentiness'. The only distinction between us is that some of us will have a greater or lesser challenge with some of these steps. Some of us will have more to 'let go of' in terms of old beliefs and inner resistance. Some of us will need to allow ourselves to dream more - bigger, more freely.

And yet we all, without exception, are capable of experiencing and enjoying *plenty.*

Nothing is static.

Change is constant.

It is *energy* that we are desiring and attracting.

<u>Where Plenty Comes From</u>

What is the Source of plenty?

Where most of us get 'tripped up' in our thinking about abundance is in our misguided assumption that everything we experience in the physical arises from the physical.

This is the first misperception that we need to overcome.

All of creation - all that we know as 'reality' - has in fact arisen from the Non-Physical universe. The Non-Physical becomes Physical, in short.

To understand - and thus open ourselves to - abundance we must expand our mind to recognize that there is a *huge* reality beyond our Physical reality. Our Physical reality is, in fact, in any given moment limited to what is 'in' it *in that moment.*

And yet nothing is static. Even in this Physical universe! Nothing is static. Therefore who you perceive yourself to be and what you 'have' - materially and spiritually - in any given moment *can and will change!* Change is a constant.

This understanding is a key in opening ourselves to abundance.

It is also vital to realize that - beyond the perceptive ability of our five Physical senses - there is an infinite reality which we cannot 'see'.

This is the reality which we tap into in creating abundance.

For everything which is not yet in the Physical - and to personalize this, anything which is not yet in *our* Physical reality - *must come to us from the Non-Physical.* Everything. Without exception. Even things which 'appear' to already exist in this Physical world. A house which we wish to buy. A car which we've test-driven. A dress, or a tuxedo, which we've seen in a shop window. A horse which ran last week at the racetrack. Even if it 'appears' to already exist in this Physical world, *we attract it through our Non-Physical experience.* We attract it to us not by 'doing'. We attract it to us by the way in which we interact with Non-Physical energy.

The attracting takes place inside of us. The allowing takes place inside of us. The receiving takes place inside of us. The *process* of abundance takes place inside of us. It is Non-Physical.

Is There Enough?

To truly appreciate the process of abundance - and the harvest of abundance - it is essential to understand that anything we desire, we attract from the Non-Physical. It is *energy* that we are desiring and attracting. And energy is limitless. It is infinite. There is more than enough energy for everyone and everything to have all of their desires fulfilled.

We exist in the heart of a bounty of supply. It is patiently waiting for us to realize it. For as we open ourselves to create and receive abundance, we inherently expand our consciousness. And as we expand our consciousness - each of us individually - human collective consciousness expands. And as we 'awaken' (a way to describe the expansion of consciousness), the nature of our desires shifts. What we want shifts.

Simply put, as more and more people awaken to the principles of abundance and begin the pilgrimage from scarcity to plenty in the multiple aspects of their lives, we will begin to recognize 'Mecca'[1]. Wanting things, desiring better health, or

---

[1] The word Mecca is often used in the English language as a metaphor for a pilgrimage site recognized by thousands of people. Derived from the

yearning for anything else which appears to be 'Physical' is a means for us to recognize the bridge between the Physical and the Non-Physical. This is the purpose of desire - to awaken us into awareness of the Non-Physical. And as we release our biases of disbelief and fear of the Non-Physical - and remember that, in fact, the Non-Physical is our 'womb', our Source of all things good - we release our limited perception of ourselves. And as we burst the seams of our limited perception of ourselves, our entire psychology shifts. We evolve, as Clare Graves elucidated, from a self-serving humanity to a whole-serving humanity.

This, if nothing else, is worth the pilgrimage to Mecca.

This, if nothing else, is worth learning how to create personal abundance 'for ourselves'.

---

name of a city in Saudi Arabia, the city of Mecca itself is revered by Muslims for containing the holiest site of Islam. A pilgrimage to Mecca is required of all able-bodied Muslims who can afford to go at least once in their lifetime.

Four Steps to Plenty

There are four rudimentary steps to achieving abundance in any area of our lives.

They are …

1. Know What You Want
2. Focus Your Attention Upon It
3. Be Aware of How You Feel
4. Get Out of The Way

When mastered, these four steps lead you to a bounty of creation each and every time. With mastery you will come to experience a great sense of relief and confidence in your understanding of these four steps and your ability to consistently follow them. Like four stone steps leading up to a temple, they will always lead you to heaven.

Each one of us, as we begin to learn and practice these steps, will find our own area of greatest challenge. This is where the 'fire of purification' is greatest for us - where the most old, accrued doubt or mis-understanding must be released and replaced with something new and functional.

Like four stone steps
leading up to a temple,
they will always
lead you to heaven.

As you begin to explore these four steps you will quickly discover which are most challenging for you.

This is where persistence comes in. And patience. And above all, practice.

You will succeed.

As you stay with these teachings, and *practice them,* you will succeed.

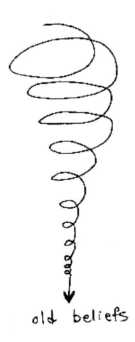

old beliefs

It can be valuable to recognize the downward spiraling 'pull' of old beliefs and old patterns of thinking and behavior. Just like the suction that pulls water down a drain. These patterns are 'ruts', meaning that there are literally 'tracks in your brain' that pull you into the grooves of your conditioning. This is why it can seem like 'hard work' to overcome them and create new ways of thinking and of behaving which lead to new results.

Think of a car that is stuck in the mud.

It often takes several runs - of rolling back, gaining momentum and determination, and revving forward - to break free of the rut.

This is as true in the Non-Physical (our mind) as it is in the Physical (the car). When you begin to realize that 'metaphysics' is simply physics in the meta (Non-Physical) realm, you will move much more swiftly on your path to awakening. On your path to *plenty.*

And so when you encounter 'mud' and you feel as if you are 'stuck', this is precisely when it is most valuable to follow these four steps and the practices therein. For these steps are the rocking back, gaining momentum and determination, and revving forward that will break you free of the old and launch you into the bounty and sheer delight of the new.

It can be very helpful, too, to find a group of people (or even just one) to practice these steps with. For your collective energy will make the rocking back, gaining momentum and determination, and revving forward so much quicker, easier and more fun.

"Life was never meant to be a struggle." - Stuart Wilde

"When did you sign a Contract to struggle?" - Ariole K. Alei[2]

Learning the steps to abundance can be fun.

And once you've learned them once, they will be with you as best friends and gifted allies forever.

This journey is worth every moment of concentration, willingness and trust that you invest into it. Start at the beginning. Stay on the path until the 'end'. And you will find a rainbow beyond your wildest dreams.

And with the tools and the confidence you gain, 'this' rainbow will be different. It will stay with you always, high in the sky, joyously lighting your way.

---

[2] I heard myself asking my students this question one evening in the midst of a Meditation Class. How profound, I thought. When *had* we signed a 'Contract' to suffer?

This journey is worth every moment of concentration,

willingness and trust that you invest into it.

Start at the beginning.

Stay on the path until the 'end'.

And you will find a rainbow beyond your wildest dreams.

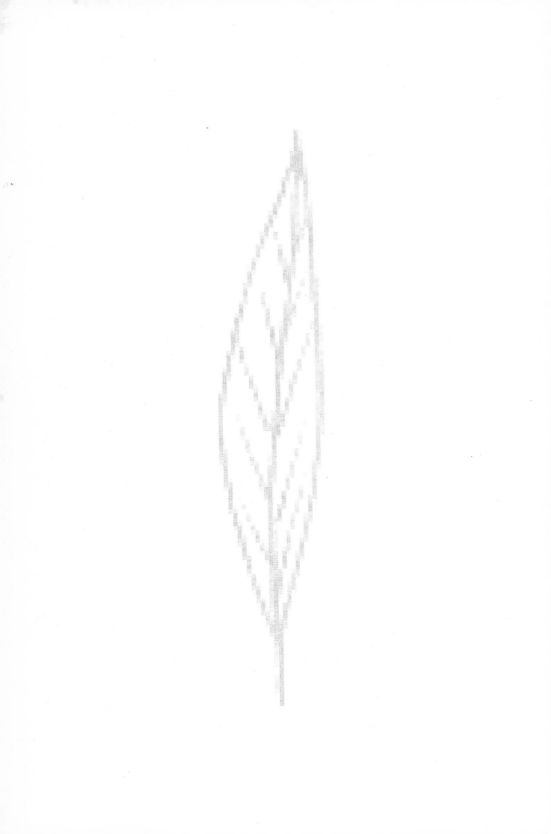

STEP 1

KNOW WHAT YOU WANT

D o you know what you want in life - right now?

If a genie were to appear to you, in this instant, and offer to grant you whatever wish you choose, would you know *in this instant* what you most want to ask for?

Some of you will say 'Yes' with delight and excitement in your voice. The opportunity of having your wish granted *now* will be like a dream come true.

Others will realize ... that they don't actually know what they want.

If this is true for you, you are not alone.

Because most people have grown accustomed to compromising on their dreams - be it their aspirations and life focus, their ideal relationship, their perfect health, or anything else that has held great meaning for them in the 'Non-Physical' (simply put, the not-yet-manifest-reality) - they have given up asking for what they want.

As soon as they fossilize into a belief that they will never get what they truly want, they stop asking.

Does this describe you?

What we're here to do, in Step 1 of creating abundance, is to understand how it is that we arise at clarity.

Clarity is a state of mind in which there is simplicity, a sense of 'knowing'. In clarity there is no ambiguity, no weighing of 'maybe this ... or maybe that'. There is a calm recognition. There is stillness.

This stillness may be coupled with excitement as we move naturally into asking for and attracting what we want. Yet the clarity itself is a state of great - and deep - calm.

How do we become clear?

One of the easiest ways to Know What We Want is through contrast. Contrast is our recognition of the *opposite* of what we *don't* want. This 'opposite' is naturally what we Do Want!

We can use our awareness of what we don't want as a powerful 'springboard'. Enjoy the ease of the journey as this 'springboard' propels us into clarity of what it is that we *do* want - that which is often an elusive 'mystery'!

Consider this:

Have you ever played 'Tiddly Winks' - a game with circular plastic chips whereby you propel one chip high through the air and way far forward by 'clicking' it with another chip?

What you don't want is the chip with which you propel the 'what you do want' chip forward.

Or in the game of pool or croquet, it is the intermediary ball with which you propel another ball to where you want it to arrive. The 'intermediary ball' is what you don't want. The ball that you 'sink' in pool or propel through the wire hoop in croquet is what you do want.

In short, we use our awareness of what we don't want *temporarily* to propel what we do want into the victory area - into our desired future. We then step into that future and it becomes our present.

Contrast – Opposite – Clarity!

Here is a very simple *contrast* exercise that will give you tremendous leverage in your path to plenty. (I am grateful to Abraham-Hicks and to Michael Losier for making this teaching so basic and rudimentary to grasp.)

Place a piece of paper horizontally in front of you.

Divide in into three vertical columns.

At the top of the left column write 'What I *Don't* Want'.
At the top of the centre column write 'What I *Do* Want'.
At the top of the right column write 'Details of *What I Want*'.

What I *Don't* Want   **What I *Do* Want**   **Details of *What I Want***

Begin with the left column. In fact, fold your paper so that this is the only column that you see.

Take as much time as you need to itemize everything that you are aware of that you don't want. Make this a thorough list.

When you feel that you've completed your left column, re-fold your paper so that now you see just the left and centre columns.

Take a moment to reflect on the items you have listed in your left column. Notice the one that draws your attention most strongly. What is its *opposite?* Write this next to it in the centre column.

Continue down your list, reflecting one at a time on what is the *opposite* of each entry you've made. And write this in the centre column next to it.

Continue until you have completed your centre column.

Then *cross out* everything in your left column. Your attention is now *completely focused on your centre and right columns.*

Fold your paper again, this time so that you only see the centre and right columns.

In this same sitting, or sometime later after you've allowed the first step of this process to gestate, contemplate each entry in your centre column. What details do you know about what you want? Write these details in your right column.

Your desired future may become manifest - seen, heard, felt, tasted, or smelled - instantly. Or it may take some time to manifest - like the Tiddly Winks chip making its slow motion arc as it travels through space.

How quickly each of your 'What I *Do* Want' desires become a Physical reality depends primarily on what resistance there is *in you* to receiving it. We'll explore this in more detail in Step 4.

Because we still live in a Physical state of duality (and in fact, until our Non-Physical and Physical selves are completely integrated and *One* again, we will continue to live in a degree of duality), we will be continuously experiencing desires.

The experience of what we don't want is a frequent occurrence each and every day of our life. This is something to celebrate! This is our Non-Physical self actively calling us to awaken to it. Every time we recognize what we don't want and, through this recognition, mindfully realize What We Do Want - and every time we mindfully shift our attention from what we don't want to our increasing clarity of What We Do Want - we are sending a 'reply' message to our Non-Physical self. We are clearly expressing to it what we would like to have 'added' to our Physical reality - our Physical experience.

State Line

Another simple way to gain insight and clarity into what we actually want is to explore it through a 'State Line'.

Find a location where you can create an unobstructed linear path of at least six feet. This could be in an enclosed room, on a beach or in a meadow, for instance. Mark each end of the path and its centre point.

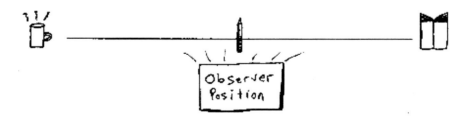

Standing 'outside of the line' and facing it as an observer, identify - in a few simple words - what each side of the line represents. For example, one side might be 'being in a wonderful, joyous relationship' and the other side might be 'being single'.

Notice which side you feel drawn to explore first.

Step onto the line at its centre point and *face your back towards* the side that you are exploring first. Begin moving slowly, a small step at a time, backward towards the end point of the line.

Notice what you feel in your body. Notice if your chest and heart centre open or close inward. Notice if you become taller or shrink downward. Notice the predominant thoughts in your mind. Notice your feelings.

Continue walking backward until you reach the marker at the line's end point.

Then step off the line to your 'observer' position facing the line's centre point. Notice what you notice internally.

Then step onto the line again at its centre point - and *face your back towards* the second side that you are about to explore. Begin moving slowly, a small step at a time, backward towards the end point of the line.

Notice what you feel in your body. Notice if your chest and heart centre open or close inward. Notice if you become taller or shrink downward. Notice the predominant thoughts in your mind. Notice your feelings.

Continue walking backward until you reach the marker at the line's end point.

Then step off the line to your 'observer' position once again. Notice what you notice internally.

What information have you gained? Which side - which option - do you feel most drawn to now?

This 'State Line' exercise accesses deep awareness and wisdom from our Non-Physical Self. It allows us to recognize more clearly What We Want.

'3 Chairs'

Another powerful tool for accessing our deep awareness - and thus positioning ourselves in a place of greater clarity to make positive choices - is '3 Chairs'.

Find a location where you can set out 3 chairs in a triangle about three feet apart.

Standing 'outside of the triangle' and facing it as an observer, identify - in a few simple words - what each of the two primary chairs represents. For example, one chair might be 'being in a wonderful, joyous relationship' and the other chair might be 'being single'. The third chair will represent your observer position - the place from which you integrate your newfound awarenesses.

Notice which of the two primary chairs you feel drawn to explore first.

Sit in it ... and notice what you notice.

Notice what you feel in your body. Notice the predominant thoughts in your mind. Notice your feelings.

Then, looking towards the other primary chair, allow yourself to ask it questions. Allow yourself to speak to it.

When you feel drawn to, switch positions - sit in the second primary chair. Notice if responses arise within you towards the first chair and the questions or comments it presented.

Allow a dialogue to begin between the two 'chairs', moving back and forth to embody each 'speaker'. Notice your inner awarenesses throughout - your sensations, thoughts and feelings.

Continue moving back and forth between the two primary chairs until you feel the conversation is complete. Then step out of the conversation to your 'observer' position - the third chair - and allow yourself to assimilate what you have witnessed.

What insights have you gained?

What new clarity do you have now to contribute to your choices?

The wise ones

who create the most abundance

with the greatest ease

know this:

The power to create lies in the

Non-Physical rather than the Physical.

<u>Doing in the Physical versus Allowing in the Non-Physical</u>

The wise ones who create the most abundance with the greatest ease know this: The power to create lies in the Non-Physical rather than the Physical.

When we attempt to create in the Physical - by doing, by action - we have available to us a *limited* array of resources with which to create. We have our past experience, things we've learned secondhand via others' experience, and the materials available to us in the Physical.

Einstein once said that we cannot solve a problem with the same thinking with which we created it.

Christian Mysticism says that if there is a problem or a lack on one level of existence we must rise 'up' to at least the next level of existence or 'vantage' to resolve it.

Physical $\rightarrow$ Emotional $\rightarrow$ Mental $\rightarrow$ Spiritual

If you are experiencing a circumstantial challenge or you desire something 'new' in the physical, you must rise at least to the emotional level of understanding to resolve it or attract it.

If you desire a better feeling emotional state, you must rise at least to the mental level of awareness to realize it.

If you are experiencing mental dis-ease or you are desiring something which is abstract, you must rise to the spiritual level of perception to attain it.

Awareness
(Spiritual)

Thoughts   (Mental)

Feelings   (emotional)

Body Sensations (Physical)

To create something that you do not yet have you must do two things:

1. Rise to a higher level of consciousness in relation to it

2. Release any resistance to receiving it

In other words, you must access your Non-Physical, limitless awareness and open yourself to grow beyond your former comfort zone.

What we have in this moment in our life represents our current comfort zone. To have anything - a thing, a quality, an experience in our life - we must be willing to *open to it*. If it doesn't already exist within the parameters of our experience, then we must, naturally, expand our parameters to receive it. We must allow our comfort zone to expand.

All bounty is fed to us

through this Vertical 'channel'.

The Four Archetypes

I would like to share with you a 'model' to assist you in understanding and practicing the two steps listed above.

Basically speaking, focusing on 'doing' and 'figuring out' in an attempt to create what we don't yet have is akin to focusing on the 'Horizontal' nature of our existence - the Physical realm in other words. Focusing our attention on our Non-Physical wealth of wisdom and capability, and on our eternal nature of Love, is akin to focusing on the 'Vertical' nature of our existence.

All bounty is fed to us through this Vertical 'channel'.

Within each of us there are four 'wisdom guides' or aspects of our consciousness who travel with us everywhere - in every moment of our waking and sleeping life. As we learn to attune to them we discover a powerful tool for directing our own life by fine-tuning it into *balance and integrity*. Conversing with our Four

Archetypes is like shaping a jelly-like substance into a refined and glowing, luminous reality.

The Four Archetypes may be one of the most valuable discoveries of your life.

Several great scholars have explored the inner landscape of the archetypes. I will share here the core four as first discovered and articulated by Carl Jung.

My beloved husband Colin Hillstrom, with whom I do much of my teaching of the Principles and Practices of Holistic Living and Loving, describes the Four Archetypes as the 'hard wiring' of the mind and the Levels of Consciousness (see Step 3) as the 'software' of the mind. Just like in a computer, there are functions within the electrical patterning of our minds that are rudimentary. These are the Four Archetypes. And there are functions within the electrical patterning of our minds which arise out of these Archetypes, like plants arising out of soil. These are our Levels of Consciousness.

<u>Your Inner King/Queen</u>

The role of the King/Queen within us is that of our Sovereign. He/she - just like a King or Queen of a monarch state - is bestowed with the role and responsibility of articulating a continuously refined Vision of our territory - our body, our thoughts, our feelings, our speech, our behavior. In short, it is our King/Queen whose function it is to clarify our life Vision.

More actively, our King/Queen *declares* this Vision *within* us and *to* us.

For instance, my inner King/Queen - my Sovereign - declares that in my territory (my life) there will be peace, prosperity, joy, laughter, abundant health, ease of motion, flowing creativity, joyous friendships, a divine relationship, a deep sense of fulfillment and purpose, honesty, integrity, truthfulness, vitality and fitness, respect, appreciation, gratitude ...

What does your King/Queen decree? Take a moment to relax, to settle the weight of your body into a comfortable chair. Allow your breath to drop deep into your belly. Savor this quiet stillness ...

Begin to notice, within you, your King/Queen. What is he/she wearing? What is the tonal quality of his/her voice? Are there words? What is his/her disposition? Is he/she lighthearted? Joyous? Self-absorbed? Where is he/she in relation to you? Hear, sense, feel or Know what he/she is decreeing for *your life.* What declarations for your well-being is he/she making?

Allow yourself to connect with your King/Queen directly - through inner eye contact, speech, an embrace, or whatever naturally arises within you.

Ask your King/Queen if he/she has a message he/she wishes to convey to you. You may receive this message as sensations, words, images, a 'knowing', or in any way it arises within you.

Receive this message, thank your King/Queen and notice that you can - anytime you choose - relax your body, let your breath sink deep into your belly, and turn your attention within - to meet your King/Queen. He/she is *always* there. In your waking and in your sleeping. Anytime you wish, you may enter within your 'self' and meet with them. Ask for their wisdom. Receive it. And thank them with generosity - gratitude expressed from your heart.

<u>Your Inner Magician</u>

The role of your Magician is to ingeniously draw the 'blueprints' of how to bring into being that which your King/Queen decrees. Your Magician is like the designer, the architect within you. The King/Queen asks for the 'house' to be built. Then the Magician sets in motion the drawing of the plans.

To design a 'house' to the King/Queen's liking and specifications (this is your 'desire'), the Magician must naturally research and explore both the known materials and the as-yet-unknown materials. The Magician must reach into the infinite realms to discover the best possible ingredients, combined in the best possible way, to create that which the King/Queen has requested.

Meeting your Inner Magician. Take a moment to relax, to settle the weight of your body into a comfortable chair. Allow your breath to drop deep into your belly. Savor this quiet stillness …

Begin to notice, within you, your Magician. What is he/she wearing? What is the tonal quality of his/her voice? Are there words? What is his/her disposition? Is he/she intently focused? Distracted? Excited? Where is he/she in relation to you? Hear, sense, feel or otherwise notice how your Magician is carrying out your King/Queen's request. Is he/she frantic? Immobile? Studious? Zanily creative? Calm and confident?

Allow yourself to connect with your Magician directly - through inner eye contact, speech, an embrace, or whatever naturally arises within you.

Ask your Magician if he/she has a message he/she wishes to convey to you. You may receive this message as sensations, words, images, a 'knowing', or in any way it arises within you.

Receive this message, thank your Magician, and notice that you can - anytime you choose - relax your body, let your breath sink deep into your belly, and turn your attention within - to meet your Magician. He/she is *always* there. In your waking and in your sleeping. Anytime you wish, you may enter within your 'self' and meet with him/her. Ask for his/her wisdom. Receive it. And give generous thanks - gratitude from your heart.

Your Inner Warrior

Your Warrior has two primary functions: to protect the territory, and to take appropriate action.

When I guide people - in groups and individually - inward to meet and converse with their Four Archetypes, it often becomes evident that their Warrior is exhausted. We live in a culture with an increasing volume and frequency of stimuli. Without effective 'screening', our Warrior becomes bombarded and overwhelmed with sorting out 'what is dangerous, what is benign, and what warrants our attention'.

In my book <u>Awakening Instinct</u> I explore and articulate for your consideration the distinction between 'real danger' and 'imagined danger'. I then take this a step further to describe what I call 'porous boundaries'.

For our Warrior to be healthy, rested, and capable of functioning at a relaxed level of high performance, he/she needs to

1. Dismantle all unnecessary 'scaffolding' - protection that was created in the past in response to a 'then' need and which has been carried around ever since

2. Learn how to - with present moment awareness (that is, not based on past experience and thus biases) - discern if a boundary needs to be created for your physical, emotional, mental or spiritual protection; conceptualize the simplest and most effective structure for that protection; create it swiftly and efficiently; notice when the 'danger' has passed; and dismantle the boundary.

In this way the Warrior can be at ease and fully rested to effectively play his/her role of protection and - equally vitally - of appropriate action.

Appropriate action is just that. It is not random action, or obsessive action, or repetitive action. It is very efficient, focused action.

When the Warrior is healthy and 'balanced', he/she has

- No unnecessary, out-dated boundaries which he/she is carrying around
- Absolute clarity as to what action is appropriate

Meeting your Inner Warrior. Take a moment to relax, to settle the weight of your body into a comfortable chair. Allow your breath to drop deep into your belly. Savor this quiet stillness ...

Begin to notice, within you, your Warrior. What is he/she wearing? What is the tonal quality of his/her voice? Are there words? What is his/her disposition? Is he/she lighthearted? Joyous? Self-absorbed? Where is he/she in relation to you? Hear, sense, feel or otherwise notice how your Warrior is carrying out the appropriate action as designed by your Magician in response to your King/Queen's Vision / desire. Is he/she exhausted? Immobile? Over zealous? Calm and confident?

Allow yourself to connect with your Warrior directly - through inner eye contact, speech, an embrace, or whatever naturally arises within you.

Ask your Warrior if he/she has a message he/she wishes to convey to you. You may receive this message as sensations, words, images, a 'knowing', or in any way it arises within you.

Receive this message, thank your Warrior, and notice that you can - anytime you choose - relax your body, let your breath sink deep into your belly, and turn your attention within - to meet your Warrior. He/she is *always* there. In your waking and in your sleeping. Anytime you wish, you may enter within your 'self' and meet with him/her. Ask for his/her wisdom. Receive it. Give thanks from the centre of your heart.

Your Inner Lover

The role of your Lover is to remind all of your other Archetypes why they are doing what they are doing. Your Lover reminds them of their meaning - their purpose, individually and collectively.

Your Lover is about Love and Life Itself.

Your Lover infuses your King/Queen, your Magician, and your Warrior with the 'fuel' of Love which keeps them focused in the direction of positive learning and benevolent growth.

Without the Guidance of your Lover's Love, the King/Queen could be a tyrant or a weakling - not a Sovereign. Your Magician could be a cruel manipulator or aloof - a 'mental masturbator' creating ideas for the sake of them. And your Warrior could be a masochist or a sado-masochist, aggressing rather than peacefully protecting and *creating*.

Meeting your Inner Lover. Take a moment to relax, to settle the weight of your body into a comfortable chair. Allow your breath to drop deep into your belly. Savor this quiet stillness …

Begin to notice, within you, your Lover. What is he/she wearing? What is the tonal quality of his/her voice? Are there words? What is his/her disposition? Is he/she lighthearted? Joyous? Self-absorbed? Where is he/she in relation to you? Hear, sense, feel or otherwise notice how your Lover is reminding your King/Queen, your Magician, and your Warrior of the essential nature of Life which is *Love.* Is he/she lethargic? Immobile? Flighty? Calm and peace-full?

Allow yourself to connect with your Lover directly - through inner eye contact, speech, an embrace, or whatever naturally arises within you.

Ask your Lover if he/she has a message he/she wishes to convey to you. You may receive this message as sensations, words, images, a 'knowing', or in any way it arises within you.

Receive this message, thank your Lover, and notice that you can - anytime you choose - relax your body, let your breath sink deep into your belly, and turn your attention within - to meet your Lover. He/she is *always* there. In your waking and in your sleeping. Anytime you wish, you may enter within your 'self' and meet with him/her. Ask for his/her wisdom. Receive it. Give thanks - from the depth of your heart.

Your Four Archetypes as Allies in Your Desires

When you take time to befriend and truly meet your own Four Archetypes, a magical process begins to quicken. The lines of communication between your Archetypes open and they begin to work together more efficiently to *co-create*. They are no longer isolated from each other. They become a 'team'. *Your* team.

There is much more to be said about the Archetypes and how you can support them into harmony to better support you. If this inspires you, contact us at info@veraxis.net.

As I mentioned earlier, there is a 'horizontal reality' - the Physical experience, and there is a 'vertical reality' - the Non-Physical experience.

Most people are taught and conditioned to work hard for what they achieve. And so they focus their life's attention on getting good skills in the body and - if they are knowledge driven - in the

When you take time to befriend
your own Four Archetypes
a magical process begins to quicken.
The lines of communication
between your Archetypes open
and they begin to work together to *co-create*.
They are no longer isolated from each other.
They become a 'team'. *Your* team.

mind. In other words, they develop their Warrior and their Magician faculties primarily. They become a Doer and/or a Thinker.

Have you ever noticed that whenever we attempt to create something 'new' with the ingredients we already have, we can - at best - create a new 'version' of the old?

To create something new - of real value - and something truly new in our experience - we must open ourselves to our King/Queen and our Lover faculties. *For it is these faculties - these Archetypes - which bridge us into the limitlessness of the Non-Physical universe.*

Our King/Queen and our Lover take us directly beyond our 'self' to our Self - the greater reality of who we are and who we can become. Our Magician and our Warrior - *if they function alone -* can only repeat what has already been.

They need the Vision of our King/Queen and the Meaning of our Lover to create something which is more valuable to us than what we currently have.

In short, if we want something that we don't yet have - an object or an experience - we must align ourselves with the Vertical reality. We must allow Non-Physical energy to enter through us into our manifest reality.

Practice is the art of repeating something sufficiently

so that it expands beyond our understanding

(a 'head' thing)

and into our experience

(a 'body' thing).

Through practice we *embody* a teaching, a principle.

And thus we discover, for ourselves, that it is real.

How Do We Open Ourselves
to the Vertical Reality?

The universe provides tremendous variety. And so there are several ways to do this.

Here are a few tools that are powerful and always effective if you commit to practice them. Practice is the art - the act - of repeating something sufficiently so that it expands beyond our understanding (a 'head' thing) and into our experience (a 'body' thing). In other words, through practice we *embody* a teaching, a principle. And thus we discover, for ourselves, that it is real.

It is through the process of making a principle real *in us* that we can begin to reap its fruits - its bountiful abundance.

The way to discover if it is *our* truth is to practice it. Through practice we 'find out'.

1. Meditate
2. Connect more frequently with your Inner King/Queen and Lover
3. Take your focus off of 'Doing' and 'Thinking' and place it on 'Visioning' and 'Loving'
4. Simply be aware of both the Non-Physical and the Physical nature of existence

Meditate

There are many ways to meditate. You can chant a mantra; focus your unwavering gaze on a candle flame; practice mindful breathing; attune your attention to the Life Force flowing in and around your body; become masterfully aware of subtle energy; watch the nature of your feelings, your sensations, and your thoughts *without engaging in them* ...

And more.

There are many, many ways to meditate.

If you would value guidance in choosing and learning ways to meditate that suit you personally, contact us at info@veraxis.net.

Here is one possibility for you ...

Breathing Like a Sponge

This process came intuitively to me one evening as I was teaching Yoga.

Here's how it goes:

Find a comfortable sitting position.

Become aware of your sitting bones beneath you. Walk them back and away from each other, creating a 'prop' - a wider base - behind you like the 'leg' at the back of a picture frame. This establishes a stable foundation for the re-creation of the natural curve of your spine.

Allow your legs to dangle, as if you're sitting on the edge of a dock.

Allow your arms to dangle, with this same feeling.

Allow your head to float upwards, like a helium balloon.

Let your eyelids gently close or partially close.

Begin to notice your breath.

Simply breathe ... observing the rise and fall of your breath ...

Begin to notice, on the In breaths, that your body is like a sponge. Thirsty for air, perhaps.

And on every In breath, it drinks the breath in fully, into every cell and every pore of your being. You are now satiating your sponge with every In breath.

Begin to notice, too, your Out breaths. Your sponge is so luxuriously full now, with the inflow of every In breath ... that it fully and completely releases the Out breath Out.

Continue breathing In ... filling every pore and cavity in your being with this blissful experience of fully drinking the breath In ...

And continue breathing Out … enjoying the vacuum which is created when you completely empty Out …

In … like a sponge, drinking the breath In …

Out … like a sponge, releasing all of the breath Out …

In …

And Out …

Fully and deliciously … like a sponge …

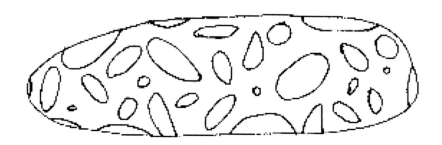

We begin to attune to something much deeper
than our thoughts. This 'something' is subtle energy.
Subtle energy is another way to describe
'Non-Physical reality'. We begin to awaken to the energy
which flows within and around us.
This … is the energy of creation.

<u>Why Meditate?</u>

Why is Meditation recommended so highly in conjunction with abundance and creating what we want in life?

Because when we meditate, we still the Warrior and the Magician and we naturally attune directly and with ease to the King/Queen and the Lover.

When we meditate, we still our body to the point that our physiological processes quieten, as if we are moving towards sleep. And yet we are more keenly, gently alert. We are temporarily surrendering our primary focus from the Physical world. We are allowing our body to deeply rest.

And when we meditate, we still our mind. Longer gaps arise between our thoughts and they hold less of our attention. We begin to attune to something much deeper than our thoughts. This 'something' is subtle energy. Subtle energy is another way to describe 'Non-Physical reality'. We begin to awaken to the energy which flows within and around us. *This* ... is the energy of creation.

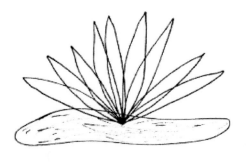

In the sweet stillness of our body and our mind, we begin to open our central channel - the internal 'shaft' which links our energy centers - our 'chakras'. And with this aligning and gradual, subtle opening of our chakras, the King/Queen of them all - our Crown chakra - begins to open. And we begin, on conscious and unconscious levels of our awareness, to align with our 'Vertical reality'. We begin to orient ourselves 'up' ... rather than 'out'.

In our sweet and increasingly inspiring stillness, we begin to taste the glow of Love within us. The divine nectar of 'God', Source, All That Is. We are 'coming Home', remembering on conscious and unconscious levels our awareness that 'God', Source, All That Is *is,* in fact, *the source* of our well-being. The source of our abundance. Of our plenty.

And with this growing experience - and increasing awareness - we shift our alignment more and more, recognizing that what we want most - what we desire - *will* come to us ... as we open ourselves 'up' ... to our 'Vertical reality'.

This new orientation is the key to allowing and receiving, in this Physical form, the manifestation of our desires.

Our desires are, in fact, our Non-Physical Self's way of leading us more and more into our fulfillment. More and more into our true nature. More and more into our Joy.

It is as if our Non-Physical Self is 'pulling us up' ... through lighting the *flame* of our desires within us.

Connecting More Frequently with your Inner King/Queen and Lover

Find a moment every day to let your body become heavy, your breath drop deep into your belly, and your attention shift to an awareness of your Inner Archetypes. This could be as you lie in bed before you rise in the morning, in your inner solitude with your eyes closed on the bus, or sitting quietly in a café as you take a break during the day.

Notice which of your Four Archetypes arises first in your awareness. As you notice it, and follow its evolution with your awareness, you will learn how to 'co-create' with it, assisting it to achieve greater balance in itself and in relation to the other three Archetypes.

If you wish assistance in developing this practice, contact us at info@veraxis.net.

The more you become familiar with each of your Four Archetypes and their relation to each other, the easier it will be for you to attune your awareness to your 'Vertical reality' - your King/Queen and your Lover.

The more you do so, the more you will open yourself - without further effort - to receiving the bounty which they will directly bring to you. This is their function, their purpose - to fill you up with Love, with Vision, with Joy.

Take Your Focus Off of 'Doing' and 'Thinking' and Place It On 'Visioning' and 'Loving'

Do you ever find yourself trying to figure things out, convinced that 'you' have to make something happen, only to become bogged down in frustration? Does this approach of 'doing' bring you the positive results that you seek?

Here's a suggestion:

Become aware, as often as you can, of when you are relying on thinking - 'figuring things out', and doing - 'making things happen' *in the absence of 'visioning' and 'loving'.*

One way to increase your awareness of this is to set your clock, watch or cell phone to 'beep' at regular intervals. This is akin to the 'bell' in some traditions of meditation. When you hear the beep - the 'bell' - notice yourself. What are you thinking? What are you doing? Are you surrendering in trust to your Lover and your

King/Queen, the Non-Physical aspects of *you* which bring bounty directly to you from its infinite Source? Or are you over-active and over-thinking?

The more you become aware of the balance - or imbalance - within you of your four Archetypes of Vision, Thinking, Doing, and Loving, the more you will be able to give your focus willfully and consciously to where the fruits of your desires *can* come from - the Non-Physical universe.

It is the role of the Physical universe (you in flesh) to receive the bounty of creation. It is the role of the Non-Physical universe (you in faith) to provide it.

It is the role of the Physical universe

(you in flesh)

to receive the bounty of creation.

It is the role of the Non-Physical universe

(you in faith)

to provide it.

Simply Be Aware of Both the Non-Physical and the Physical Nature of Existence

I often suggest to my meditation students that they consider life to be a 'PhD thesis' - that they explore life with such a curiosity that they could, if they chose to, articulate the fine details of their discoveries to another person.

Why not make your awareness of the reality, distinction, and connection between the Physical and the Non-Physical universe your 'PhD thesis' and place your attention upon it?

Why not be like a child, curious and insatiable in your inquiry?

Why not focus your attention on learning this - *through your direct experience?*

Here is an example of how this might sound …

"Hmm. This is interesting. My thoughts aren't physical! And yet I have assumed that they were a part of my 'Physical' reality because I associate them with being in a body.

"Hmm. This is interesting. My feelings aren't physical! And yet I have assumed that they were a part of my 'Physical' reality because I associate them with being in a body.

"Hmm. This is interesting! When I focus my attention on my breath, my mind becomes very still and calm.

"Hmm. This is interesting! The clouds waft and move, transforming their shapes in the sky. I have thought of them before as being physical. Are they?

"Hmm. What is in this 'air', this 'space' between me and the tree I am looking at 'over there'?

"Hmm. Someone just said something to me. Is communication physical? Are words physical?

"Hmm. This is very interesting. I'm beginning to get a sense of how the Physical and the Non-Physical are interfacing all the time. How the Non-Physical is always here, present in the Physical, co-existing with it.

"Wow. This is exciting! What else 'exists' that I haven't noticed yet?"

Simplexity - Summary So Far

To receive what we want, we must Know What We Want - we must have clarity of what we are asking for. One of the easiest ways to gain this clarity is through contrast - recognizing that the opposite of what we *don't* want is the nature of what we *do* want.

Anything that we don't yet have must come to us from the Non-Physical.

A powerful way to connect with our Non-Physical Self is through Meditation.

Meeting our Four Inner Archetypes assists us to recognize the powerful inner guides and mentors within us who travel with us everywhere, all the time.

Shifting our primary attention from 'doing' and 'thinking' to 'visioning' and 'loving' opens us up to our Non-Physical Self.

The more we are aware of both the Non-Physical and the Physical nature of reality, the more we are in the *flow* of receiving what we want.

STEP 2

FOCUS YOUR ATTENTION UPON IT

Your power - your only *true* power - is in
this moment, now.

For some people, Knowing What You Want is the greatest challenge in the process of abundance. Once you know what you want, the rest flows into place with ease.

If this describes you, practice the suggestions in the previous chapter until a 'Vision' opens up for you. You will know it as soon as you perceive it, as you will be filled with a sudden Joy and Excitement ... because you are feeling the coming 'towards' you of something new. It is traveling towards you in time. Just like the shift in ions in the air before a rain, you will sense that something wonderful is on its way to you.

The second step in creating abundance of any kind is to Focus Your Attention Upon It - your Vision, your desire, that which you now Know That You Want.

Just like an Olympic athlete or a concert musician,

it is practice that 'grooves' the electrical pathways

in your brain to make *this*

the dominant response within you.

You literally have moved into a new terrain in entering step two, as it is no longer about discerning clearly what you don't want, or 'test driving' what you think you do want in your future.

With this second step, you are truly and really in the *now*.

As you master this second step, you will master what all religious and spiritual teachings point to: Your power - your only *true* power - is in this moment, now.

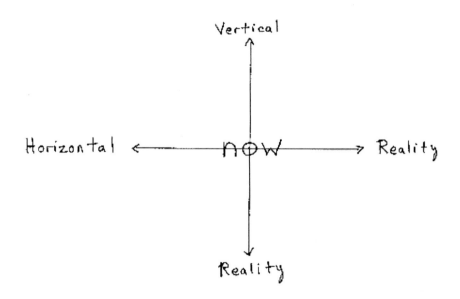

You cannot create from the future perspective, or from the past. *Because it is in this moment now that the Vertical and the*

Horizontal realities meet. The only 'connecting' point for them to 'touch' each other is **now.**

Focusing Your Attention Upon It may sound easy. It is, once you gain the mental discipline to do this. Just like an Olympic athlete, or a concert musician, it is practice that 'grooves' the electrical pathways in your brain to make *this* the dominant response within you.

The reason - the one and only reason - why most people find it difficult to create what they want in life is that they are focused - aware or unaware, consciously or unconsciously - on what they don't want.

Listen to people around you. The majority of people are talking about what they *don't* want and *don't* like. Have you ever noticed this?

By giving their attention to this, they are attracting more of it *by the Law of Attraction.* This, like all Natural Laws, is universal and consistent. It is not selective - it applies to everyone, all the time.

If you want more love, focus on love in your life. Think about love. Express gratitude for the love you have. Imagine having even more love. *But as soon as you begin to spiral downward into thinking about the love you 'don't' have, you must stop and recognize where your attention is directed.* Just like a train engine in a roundhouse, re-establish your clarity about which track leads toward the results you seek. Then get on that track.

You will get on that track, simply, easily and efficiently, by focusing on what you have, what you love, and what you want more of.

What I Have ...

_____

_____

_____

_____

_____

What I Love …

_____

_____

_____

_____

_____

What I Want More Of …

_____

_____

_____

_____

_____

The longer and more consistently you focus your attention upon what you want, the swifter it will come into being in your Physical experience.

It's just like tending a garden. The more attention you give to removing the weeds (your thoughts on what you *don't* want); the more you water it and fertilize it and appreciate it and envisage the plants growing strong and tall and fragrant and fruitful (focusing your attention on what you *do* want); the more quickly and richly your garden will grow.

With focus - attention - there is a powerful principle that must be understood: **What we focus on grows.**

And so if we are focusing, even unwittingly, on our perceived miseries and lack *rather than using this awareness as a springboard for clarity of what we* ***do*** *want,* then we will create more of what we don't want by default.

The power of our focus - our attention - is key in our ability to create our desires.

In my book <u>Awakening Instinct</u> I describe the 'Psychic Undertow' which keeps us from growing and evolving, as individuals and collectively. As Don Miguel Ruiz describes so eloquently in <u>The Mastery of Love</u>, we must develop such an inner power that we propel ourselves right through that downward spiral, surfacing 'above the soil' as the new sprout, the seed of something fresh and vibrant.

The power to 'break through'
resides in consistently practicing this:
Noticing what we are giving our attention to.

The power to 'break through' comes from consistently practicing this: Noticing what we are giving our attention to.

Here are some ideas to assist you to 'break through' ...

- Value What You Want
- Express Gratitude
- Write 'My Attention Journal'
- Use a Reminder Bell
- Create a Vision Board or Box
- Declare Affirmations
- Converse with my Non-Physical Self

You may have other ideas to add to this list. If you would like to share them with us, please do so at info@veraxis.net. We always appreciate learning new 'tools' to practice and teach to our clients and readers. Thank you!

Value What You Want

The most important first step in getting what we want is to *value* what we want.

Look around you in your life. Notice what you already have and enjoy. Notice what you don't have, yet have a feeling of desire for.

What do you value?

Do you honestly value what you don't yet have?

If you are truthful and honest with yourself you may recognize that that which you want, yet don't have, you don't yet *value* as highly as that which you already have.

This lack of valuing can stem from so many sources - from cultural upbringing, to gender upbringing, to family values, to childhood experiences of wanting and not getting - and convincing yourself that "it's not really important".

What I am suggesting to you here is that, if you want something, do a personal inner inventory to see if you really do value it.

You can discover this clarity in ways such as ...

- Notice how you speak about what you want. What do you say? How do you *feel* when you say it?
- Notice how you look at what you want.
- Notice how you feel when you think about what you want.

We can think we want something and truly want it - and not value it.

So ... how can you value more that which you want?

Here are a few suggestions ...

Use the Power of your words and thoughts (see 'The 12 Soul Powers' in Step 4) to affirm how much you appreciate the nature of what you want.

Use your Imagination thoughts (see 'The 12 Soul Powers' in Step 4) to see yourself interacting with ease, openness and receptivity to what you want.

Put a 'bit of what you want' in a place where you will see it, at a relaxed time of your day, every day. Focus Your Attention Upon It. Open your heart. Notice any feelings of anxiety or resistance in you. Hold this 'symbol of what you want' to your heart, and then to your forehead. Then place it where you will see it again later, or tomorrow.

Express Gratitude

Expressing gratitude - even for something you *apparently* don't yet have - is a powerful way to open yourself to receiving it.

Gratitude dissolves resistance and acknowledges and affirms value.

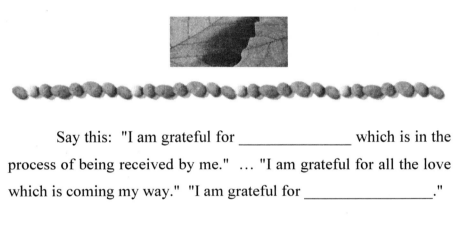

Say this: "I am grateful for _____ which is in the process of being received by me." ... "I am grateful for all the love which is coming my way." "I am grateful for _____."

Imagine how your life would be ... if you expressed gratitude a million times a day, lovingly acknowledging everything you experience as beautiful, generous, and wonder-full!

Step out and overcome your 'shyness'. Thank everyone and everything that makes even a moment in your day brighter, lighter and more joyous.

Actively do this: Develop a practice of thankfulness, gratitude, and over-flowing appreciation.

Say 'Thank You' often and abundantly.

Open your heart. Express your love.

Do you notice how your day unfolds effortlessly in the 'tone' of this golden path? You 'pave the way'. You create an abundance of gratitude with this simple seed you express.

Create momentum with your gratitude!

Write 'My Attention Journal'

Create your own special journal with re-cycled paper or purchase a journal whose color, texture and 'feel' appeal to you. Choose a pen or colored pencil that you feel inspired to write with. Design a way to carry these easily with you - wherever you go.

Whenever you become 'conscious in the present moment', notice what you are giving your attention to. And write this down. Without judgment or censoring, write this down. (Purchase a journal with a lock, if you prefer!)

Every few days take a few moments to review what you have recently written. Notice the themes. Has your focus been relaxed, peaceful, or excited? Has it been directed to things which you are worried about? Has it been forceful, endeavoring to get its own way through manipulation? Has it been indulging in thoughts which feel dishonest or troubled? Has it been joyous and free?

It's never too late to get back on track.

Notice both the *nature* of your attention and the *content* of your attention.

Have you been thinking the same thoughts over and over again? Have you shied away from thoughts, feeling insecure or embarrassed about their subject matter?

Have you been focusing your attention on what you want? Or on what you don't want? Have you been complaining - audibly or inaudibly? Have you been blaming?

If you have been complaining or blaming, you have been disempowering yourself. If this is happening for you, as soon as you become self-aware - aware that you are blaming or complaining - immediately and intentionally shift your attention to *what you do want*.

It's never too late to get back on track.

Focus your attention on what you do want.

Use a Reminder Bell

As mentioned in step one - Know What You Want - a 'reminder bell' can be an excellent tool for bringing your awareness into the present moment. In the present moment, you can 'self observe'.

Set your clock, or watch, or cell phone to beep at regular intervals. Just like the 'bell' in some meditation traditions, use this 'alerting' signal to bring your awareness to what you have most recently been focusing on.

Just notice.

If what you have been focusing on is *not* what you want, then use this moment of realization to switch tracks - to switch direction - with your engine. Mindfully, intentionally engage your thoughts, speech, and imagination on what you *do* want.

If what you've been focusing on *is* what you want, celebrate! Congratulate yourself! Acknowledge to yourself your recognition that you are moving solidly and truly in the direction of creating in the Physical that which you do want.

It is with Attention Upon It that our Non-Physical Self channels through us the energy to attract, create, and receive anything and everything that we ask for.

So be more diligent about what you shine the light of your attention upon. Your attention is like greenhouse lights. No matter whether you are awake or asleep, the 'greenhouse lights' continuously foster the growth of that upon which they shine.

Imagine that your mind is like a camera lens —
a photo or a movie camera. In fact, it is a *zoom* lens.
And you are the photographer.

Become aware that it is you who shifts
the direction of the lens. It is you
who determines where you place your focus.

'Zoom In, Zoom Out'

I found myself spontaneously creating this Meditation Tool while teaching a corporate meditation class. It is a powerful way to take sovereign, co-creative control of where our attention is focused.

Imagine that your mind is like a camera lens - a photo or a movie camera. In fact, it is a *zoom* lens. And you are the photographer.

With your eyes closed, allow your attention - your zoom lens - to shift to the outside world. Notice in detail the sounds you hear, the light you see through your closed eyelids, the aromas you smell, the flavors you taste, and the sensations and vibrations you feel against your skin. Pay precise attention to the details of information - the stimuli - around you.

When you feel ready to ... turn your camera lens ... '180°' ... so that you begin to observe your *inner* world. Notice the inner sounds, inner visual awarenesses, inner sensations, inner aromas and tastes, inner 'knowings'. Pay precise attention to the details of information - the stimuli - within you.

When you feel ready to … shift your awareness to the outer world again. Notice what you notice.

Then shift your awareness to the inner world again. Notice what you notice.

Continue shifting the focus of your lens from the inner to the outer world as frequently or infrequently as you feel drawn to, *becoming aware that it is you who shifts the direction of the lens.* It is you who determines where you place your focus.

Continue shifting the focus of your lens from the inner to the outer world, recognizing *how* you are doing this. Continue until the path - the process - feels natural and easy to you.

Then rest.

Allow your lens to rest as you integrate what you have experienced.

What did you discover? What did you notice? Do you recognize now that you are the 'photographer' in every moment of your life?

It's true. It is you and only you who decides where you place your focus. Make this a *conscious* choice - and you will move a giant step towards making your desires real in the Physical reality.

Make this a *conscious* choice –
and you will move a giant step towards making your
desires real in the Physical reality.

Create a Vision Board or Box

Most things that people want can be represented by pictures - whether they be 'things' or 'people' or 'qualities'.

The magnetism of your King/Queen's Vision can be greatly fortified by your creating a descriptive picture of what you want.

Choose a box that you feel drawn to. Or a large piece of colored paper. If you've chosen a box, decorate it if you wish.

Then, over the course of the next few days, keep your eyes open for images that represent that which you desire.

As you refine your awareness of images that represent to you that which you desire, seek images that you can place in your box or on your large piece of colored paper. Great sources are magazines, flyers, brochures, travel brochures, images that you can download and print from the internet, photographs, your own drawings, and whatever else you find that works for you.

Create a collage on your large piece of colored paper - or simply place the images in your box. Know that everything you are including in your collage or your box will, in its essence, come to you. *If you Focus Your Attention Upon It.*

So place your completed box or collage somewhere where it is easily accessible to you. (You can always add to it, anytime you like.)

Now pull out your day-timer or calendar. Put a circle around the same day of the week for the next two months. In that circle write 'box' or 'collage' to remind you what the circle is for.

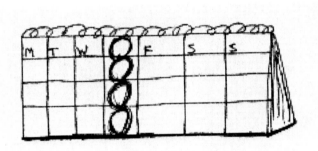

When the next circle day arrives, take out your box or collage - and breathe slowly and deeply as you look, with leisure and relaxation, at all that you have placed there. If something strikes you as no longer fitting your Vision, remove it. If you have new clarity of something that needs to be added, add it.

Do this every time a circle day arrives.

And notice what happens!

Declare Affirmations

Affirmations are one of the most powerful ways to Focus Your Attention Upon Want You Want.

It is *very important* that your affirmations are believable to you. If they aren't, they will instill doubt and will actually counteract your easy creation of your desires. We will explore this in more detail in Step 3.

To create a simple *and effective* affirmation, articulate in a few words something that you want.

Then ask yourself: Do I believe that this can come true?

You will *feel* your response to this. Either you will feel excited and energized - or you will feel a sinking feeling in your stomach. This is your own personal version of noticing what 'spirals you up' and what 'spirals you down'.

If your affirmation excites and energizes you, you've got it!

If it makes you feel wheezy and uncertain, then scale it down. Make it 'smaller'. Less adventurous. A little closer to your current situation, now.

Then speak this new affirmation to yourself.

Again ask yourself: Do I believe that this can come true? And notice how you feel.

If your affirmation excites and energizes you now, you've got it!

If not, scale it down again. Repeat this process until you've articulated an affirmation that *makes you feel* **great**.

Once you've found your great feeling affirmation, reflect for a moment on your average day. When would be good times to remind yourself of your affirmation and speak it silently to yourself or aloud? Be innovative, as if you're a project designer, finding the best places to instill power into your affirmation throughout your day.

Repeat this process

until you've articulated an affirmation that

makes you feel **great**.

Once you've found good times for it, notice how you will remind yourself to speak your affirmation. There are many options that could work for you.

Here are a few ideas ...

1.   Write it on a card beside your bed so that it is the first thing you see when you wake up in the morning

2.   Write it on tiny (or not so tiny!) pieces of paper and post them around your house, in your briefcase or handbag, on your coffee or tea mug, inside the fridge - wherever you will see it easily *at the times you have designated throughout your average day*

3.   Record it on a voicemail and call yourself to hear yourself speak it

4.   Memorize it, then choose a 'code word' which represents it. Place this code word in numerous locations along your daily 'trail'

5.   In other words, gently and lovingly *surround yourself* with the energy of your affirmation. In this way, you won't just 'think' it. You will *become* it.

Can you see how these steps might support you on your chosen path?

<u>Converse With My Non-Physical Self</u>

Most of us have been taught to believe that conversing with ourself - or anyone who isn't visible - means that 'we're crazy'.

Are we crazy *not* to speak with our Non-Physical Self?

Just like you would set a date to speak with a friend or a special time with your beloved, your parent, or your child, it is absolutely vital if you wish to create something which you do not yet have that you begin to converse with your Non-Physical Self.

For it is your Non-Physical Self who will deliver this desire to you.

It is your Non-Physical Self who will fill you with wisdom about what *you* need to do - or cease doing - in the Physical in order to make room for this new desire to arrive.

To ignore your Non-Physical Self is to ignore your greatest mentor. It is like expecting to live a fully functioning life while being deaf to the greatest source of wisdom that you have.

You allow your Non-Physical Self

to lift you closer

to where you can receive what it is that you desire.

How do you strike up a conversation with your Non-Physical Self?

It doesn't need to be loud. It doesn't even need to be in words. It can simply be you, strolling along on a path in the woods, knowing that your 'companion' on this walk is your Non-Physical Self. And as you stroll along, you open yourself easily and naturally to non-verbal, unspoken communication. You allow this to enrich you, to comfort you, to assure you, to align you with what you want. You allow it to lift you closer to where you can receive it.

You can 'converse' with your Non-Physical Self as you take a bath. Or as you sit in silence, curled up in your favorite chair, with a mug of herbal tea that calms your nervous system.

You can 'converse' with your Non-Physical Self as you are awed by great symphonic or instrumental music.

What connects you with your Non-Physical Self –

always –

is gratitude.

The 'carrier' for this conversation can be anything, any place that soothes you, that quiets you. For it is in this tranquility that you can most easily connect - that you can most easily begin to recognize - the *presence* of your Non-Physical Self.

What connects you with your Non-Physical Self, always, is gratitude.

<u>Simplexity - Summary So Far</u>

Once we have clarified What We Want, just like a gardener tending a garden, we must Focus Our Attention Upon It.

To receive what we want, we must value it.

When we declare affirmations - from the voice of our sovereign, our King/Queen - these affirmations must be *believable to us*.

To create What We Want, we must ensure that Our Attention Is Focused Upon It. Most people create more of what they *don't* want *because this is what they are focusing on, talking about, and thinking about.*

There are many ways to Focus Our Attention Upon What We Do Want - like shining light upon, and sprinkling water upon, and feeding nutrients to - a seed.

Some of these include Creating a Vision Board or Box, Using a Reminder Bell, and Conversing With My Non-Physical Self.

What we focus on grows.

STEP 3

BE AWARE OF HOW YOU FEEL

What are feelings?
What is their purpose?

Feelings are
the most tangible way
that we can receive
moment-to-moment communication
from our *Non-Physical Self.*

T here are people who are not aware of their feelings - they don't know what they are feeling, even if they turn their attention to what they *might* be feeling.

There are others who are distraught by the relentlessness of their downward spiraling feelings or the imbalanced 'swinging' nature of their upward spiraling feelings.

What are feelings?

What is their purpose?!?

Have you ever considered this? The purpose of your feelings?

Feelings are perhaps the most profound way that subtle energy can be processed by the 'basic model, average human'. I say 'basic model, average human' meaning someone who has not developed a specialized awareness of subtle energy to any degree, through martial arts, meditation, yoga, tantra, observation of nature, or any other path of discovery.

We all experience feelings, whether we are aware of them or not. An absence of awareness of one's feelings suggests an over-balance of the Magician - that is, thinking to the degree that our awareness of our feelings is over-ridden.

Feelings are the most tangible way that we can receive the moment-to-moment communication from our *Non-Physical Self.* Feelings are how our Non-Physical Self communicates with us.

This "Emotional Guidance System" is so clearly articulated in the teachings of Abraham as received and presented by Esther and Jerry Hicks. (See page 114 in <u>Ask and It Is Given</u>.) Each of us is born with a complete and perfectly functioning "EGS".

Our feelings are a direct compass needle showing us where we are - at any nano-second in time - within the 17 Levels of Consciousness (see page 104).

Simply put, when we feel happiness, joy, or any 'good' feeling, this is our Non-Physical Self confirming that we are on track - on course to creating in the Physical that which we desire.

The degree of our feeling good - optimism to glee, for instance - is the subtle communication of our Non-Physical Self to us, our Physical self. Optimism, if accurately 'read' by us - like reading the mercury level of a thermometer - would tell us that we are focused toward the creation of our desire ... yet there is still some degree of doubt or uncertainty within us. Glee, accurately 'read' by us, would tell us that we are completely welcoming and allowing the arrival of our desire, with no resistance whatsoever.

In a state of glee, "bring it on, baby" is a message ringing true from our every cell. We are ready, on all levels of our being, for our desire to be born.

When we feel sadness, grief, guilt, or any other 'bad' feeling, this is our Non-Physical Self telling us, loud and clear (if we know how to read it), that we are *off track*. *It is time to re-direct our engine. To re-fine our focus.*

And yet, because most of us have not understood how to interpret these signals from our Non-Physical Self, we have not heeded them. We have continued in the off-direction of our train, suffering in greater and greater misery, confused about 'what is going wrong'.

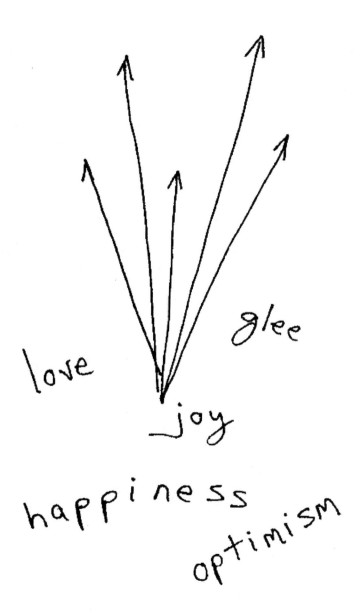

So the good news is: Pay attention to your feelings! Recognize the quality of your present feeling. Is it spiraling you upward? Does it feel good? Could it feel better? Are you ready to think a thought that produces an even better feeling - now?

Or is it spiraling you downward? Does it feel bad? If so, in Abraham's words, "Reach for a better feeling thought." Try out a whole closet full of thoughts if you need to - until you find one that gives you a feeling of *relief.* This relief is a signal that you have begun - a little or a lot - to spiral *up.*

The 17 Levels of Consciousness

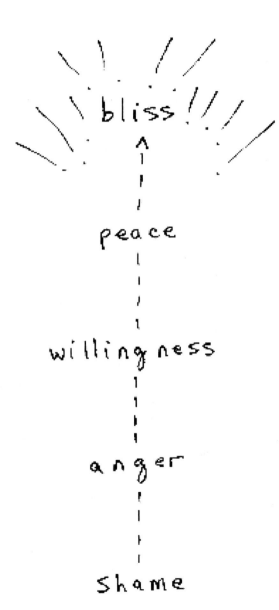

There have been several great thinkers in recent times - people who have used their faculty of thinking to observe, to question, to notice and recognize patterns in 'nature' which they then teach as tools to others - teachers who have focused their precious time and life attention to 'mapping' the levels of human conscious-ness. One of these is Dr. David Hawkins.

Similar to Abraham's 22 level "Emotional Guidance System", Hawkins' 17

Level "Map of Consciousness" gives us a clear map of how the human emotional states relate to each other. In other words - as in the children's song "the foot bone is connected to the ankle bone" - which emotion leads to which.

To view Hawkins' 17 Level "Map of Consciousness" see pages 68-69 in his book <u>Power vs Force</u>.

In our private practice we guide our clients through a 'C-Walk' - a Consciousness Walk in which they experience, in a deeply profound way, their own 17 Levels of Consciousness. With familiarity *in their felt experience* of these 17 Levels they are then much more adept at navigating their way *at will* into higher levels - more enjoyable states - of consciousness, or 'feeling'. If this inspires you, contact us at <u>info@veraxis.net</u>.

Either of these systems - or any other similar system - allows us, in any given moment - to

1. Recognize where we are on the emotional 'scale'
2. Decide whether this is truly where we want to be
3. With a little bit of practice, willfully move ourselves to somewhere more enjoyable

Ask yourself this:

How would I like to feel, in this moment?

Recognize the answer that comes.

Simply put, our outer experience is filtered through our inner experience - *our emotions.*

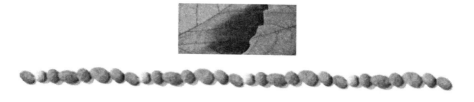

Here's how it works:

Pause, precisely where you are, and reflect for a moment. How do you feel? (For some people this recognition will take some practice.) Ashamed? Humiliated? Guilty? Apathetic? Sad? Fearful? Angry? Lustful? Full of pride? Courageous? Neutral? Accepting? Willing and open? Understanding? Loving? Joyous? Peaceful? Blissful?

Is this how you would like to feel? Does it feel *good?* Is this feeling state energizing? Pleasing? Comforting? A relief?

If not, ask yourself this: How would I like to feel, in this moment?

Recognize the answer that comes.

Then, looking at either Abraham's 22 level "Emotional Guidance System", Hawkins' 17 Level "Map of Consciousness", or another system which works equally well for you, *position yourself where you want to be.* See yourself feeling this new emotion. Hear yourself speaking with this new emotion singing in your voice. Feel yourself moving with ease and relaxation from this new emotion.

In other words, *choose* it. Willfully choose how you want to feel.

Deciding

Most of us, without recognizing it, follow the flock as if we are sheep. We are conditioned and cultured in ways that disempower us and keep us well below living our true potential. (See Don Miguel Ruiz's <u>The Four Agreements</u> and my <u>Running the Gauntlet</u> which is the second section of <u>Awakening Instinct *Running the Gauntlet * Windows Through Time</u> if this draws your attention.)

We naively are asleep to the fact that *we can decide.*

The power of deciding is overlooked by many, many people.

You have the power within you, in any moment in time, to decide how you want to feel, through what color eyes you want to see the world - how you want to 'be'.

Just decide.

"I want to feel happy, now."

"I will feel happy, now."

"I feel happy, now."

Try this series of statements with any emotional state you wish to move into. The *sequence* of these statements is essential. For you must align your *will* as the 'bridge' between what you want and what you are.

Deciding is very powerful.

Decide anything … and notice what happens.

<u>Get On the Merry Go Round</u>

One of the many valuable practices taught in the Abraham-Hicks books, CDs and DVDs is 'Getting on the Merry Go Round'.

If you recall our exploration of Affirmations in the Focus Your Attention Upon It chapter of this book, you'll remember that to be effective, Affirmations must be believable *to you.*

In order to shift into a better feeling state by choosing a better feeling thought (try it - change your thought and you change your feeling state), you must choose a thought that 'sticks' - a thought *that you can believe.*

Here's how it works:

As soon as you notice that you are feeling anything less than happy, relaxed and at ease, pause and reflect. Notice the predominant thought that you have been thinking. *This thought has propelled your feeling state in the direction of suffering.*

To get 'back on track' in the direction of feeling good, you need to simply choose a better feeling thought.

Take a moment. Allow another thought to float up into your awareness. How does it make you feel? Better? If so, keep thinking it. Worse? If so, allow another thought to float up into your awareness. Keep doing this until you find a thought that truly shifts you into feeling better. Then continue to think it. Focus your attention on this thought until this new, better feeling state is anchored within you.

Inner Thinking, Outer Thinking

To create what we want - that is, to allow and receive *into* our Physical experience that which apparently doesn't yet exist – we must align our Inner Thinking and our Outer Thinking.

Reflect on someone whom you know quite well. What is their general outlook? Are the words they speak and the comments they make typically inspiring or of a complaining nature?

Then, if you know them really well, reflect on what you've observed about their relationship with themselves. What is your sense of their inner talk?

Sometimes it is easier to explore a new idea 'outside of ourselves'.

So now, having pondered upon the Outer Thinking and the Inner Thinking of someone you know quite well, ponder upon your own Outer Thinking and Inner Thinking.

To create what we want,
we must align our Inner Thinking and our Outer Thinking.

What is the outlook
through which you generally perceive the world?

What is the nature of the silent thoughts,
spoken within you?

What is the outlook through which *you* generally perceive the world? Do you see beauty and opportunity around you? How do you typically engage with other people? In a joyous, friendly, appreciative way? Or with distrust, criticism and blame?

Once you've pondered this awhile and have a sense of your Outer Thinking, turn your attention inward and begin to reflect upon your Inner Thinking.

What is the nature of the silent thoughts, spoken within you? Are you trusting that good experiences will come your way? Are you secretly suspicious, or judgmental, or spiteful?

To attract and allow and receive what we want to bring into our lives, we must find harmony between our Inner Thoughts and our Outer Thoughts. Without this, they contradict each other and 'cancel our desires out'.

What to do:

Take reflective moments frequently to observe and become more keenly aware of how you interact with the world (your Outer Thinking) and how you interact with yourself (your Inner Thinking). You might 'Use a Reminder Bell' to assist you with this practice.

Notice the discrepancies.

Then practice choosing a better feeling thought in whichever arena it is needed. Do this until you can feel the harmony - like two notes singing together - of your Inner Thinking and your Outer Thinking working *together* to co-create the results you want. These results are your desires. Get both your Inner Thinking and your Outer Thinking working together for you, and you will have certainty guaranteed that you will realize your dreams.

Doubt

Doubt is the primary reason why people who 1. Know What They Want and 2. Focus Their Attention Upon It become frustrated at their slow or apparently non-existent results.

Doubting is like having the brakes on and trying to move forward at the same time.

Doubt negates our best intentions and our strongest desires.

When doubt is present it will be much harder to 'climb the mountain' … and there will be a much greater likelihood that we will tire before we reach the top.

So how do we recognize if we are doubting? And what do we do about it?

It is easy to recognize when we know how.

Doubting

is like having the brakes on

and trying to move forward

at the same time.

Say your Affirmation. Notice your breathing. Is it deep? Does your body relax? Do you feel relief? Do you feel the inner warmth of peace?

If you answer Yes to any of these questions, then doubt is either not present or it is on its way out - it is being dissolved by your *inner knowing,* your growing belief that what you want, you can have.

If you answer No to any of these questions, then re-word your Affirmation as described in the previous chapter until your breath deepens as you speak it, your body relaxes, and you feel an inner warmth of relief and peace. These are signals that you *believe what you are saying.*

Doubt arises from one of the deepest mis-understandings in human beings - that we are somehow unworthy of love, of joy, of plenty.

When you grasp this –

when you really 'get it' –

that you have always been whole,

that you have always been held in the loving arms of

plenty –

then you will begin to allow yourself

to have and to create

all that you desire.

This mis-perception of un-deservingness usually stems from a traumatic or chronic experience which overwhelmed us, frightened us, or confused us. Without the consciousness tools to understand that what happened (or what we perceived happened) was in no way a reflection of our worthiness, we allow a perceptual cut to enter into our sense of ourselves. This is the only way that we can make sense, at the time, of what happened.

And so, when this happens, we carry - deep within us and beneath our conscious awareness - a belief that we are not good enough. That we are not whole. That we aren't deserving. That we can't have what we most truly want.

To flip this mis-perception and thus create what we want, we must recognize this mis-understanding for what it is.

Connect with your Non-Physical Self again. Your Non-Physical Self is whole and has always been whole - and will always be whole. Your Non-Physical Self has never experienced lack and never will experience lack. To your Non-Physical Self, deserving is

There is no lack. Anywhere.

Or in you.

There never has been.

not a question. Deserving is a concept that it knows nothing about. Because it has never been 'undeserving'. And neither have you.

When you grasp this - when you really 'get it' - that you have always been whole, that you have always been held in the loving arms of plenty - then you will begin to allow yourself to have and to create all that you desire. You will allow yourself to *live* Love and *be* Love.

There is no lack. Anywhere. Or in you.

There never has been.

How Do I Want to Feel Afterwards?

When I was a professional dancer I 'intuitively knew' several processes which brought so much joy and fulfillment into my life.

I noticed, in my early performing years, that most of my veteran colleagues were near to vomiting with anxiety backstage.

I realized that fear and excitement are *the same energy* on two sides of a continuum. And so I realized that, with the recognition of fear, this energy could be 'transmuted' into its counter-part - excitement.

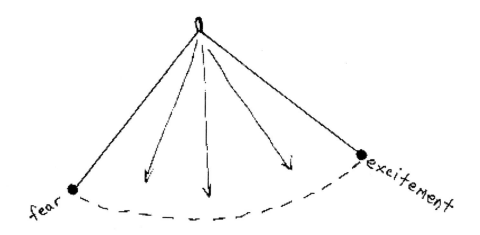

Immediately, I knew how to do this.

I just ... 'put my energy ... on the side of the continuum of excitement'. And immediately I felt joy, ease, and the thrill of anticipation of the performance I was about to dance.

Try it.

When you recognize that you are feeling fear, 'put your energy ... on the side of the continuum of excitement'.

And notice what happens!

I also became intuitively aware of this: I began to ask myself, "How do I want to feel *after* the performance?" And I envisioned myself the morning after, in the quiet of my hotel room, enjoying the warm afterglow of the night before as if a sun was rising inside my own body.

Simply put, I recognized how I wanted to feel *afterwards*.

And this is *always* how I felt.

What had I done? How had I done this? It was like 'magic', as if I had 'decided' how I wanted to feel - *and then I felt it!*

It was that simple. I paused, and took a moment to become clear about WHAT I WANTED. In this case, it was how I wanted to feel 'after' something took place.

This effectively 'paved the way for my experience'. It set in motion the circumstances required *in me* for me to reach my desired outcome. *Effortlessly.*

That is the beauty of Deciding How You Want to Feel Afterwards. It makes the journey to that state of being absolutely effortless.

Try it.

Take a moment to clarify What You Want - How You Want to Feel After some event or aspect of your day. Then let go. And notice, later, how it has unfolded to carry you, absolutely effortlessly, to fulfilling your desire.

Experiential Rehearsals

I also became intuitively aware of a process which I call 'Experiential Rehearsals'.

When I toured internationally with dance companies we would typically have several hours to rest after rehearsal at the theatre and before we would do our make-up, warm up, and dress in our costumes for the performance.

During this time most of my colleagues would sleep.

I would lie on my hotel bed - though I wouldn't sleep.

I would see, in my inner mind, the fine details of my performance - the pre-setting of my costumes for rapid costume changes, my entrances and exits, and the precision movements of my performance.

I would notice that, during this process, what I was seeing was the 'bones' of the performance.

I would then listen to a particular piece of music which would infuse my entire being with Love. I would feel as if I was floating in this beauteous sea of Love.

My colleagues would be awake by then and we would be transported back to the theatre. They would do their preparations amidst nervous chatter. I would, from the stillness of my inner being, prepare in silence and a glorious sense of calm.

This process of 'Experiential Rehearsals' became incredibly valuable when I began to tour as a solo artist. With just me on the stage, preparing and performing with utter confidence made this experience a continuous joy.

I learned, through this experience, that what I was seeing in my inner awareness was the performance flawlessly unfolding in the Non-Physical realms. It 'had already happened'! All I had to do then was to warm up my body and allow it to happen once again, this time in the Physical. I understood from this 'teaching' that we can pave the way in the Non-Physical for experience to happen effortlessly and joyously in the Physical.

I learned, through this experience,

that what I was seeing in my inner awareness

was the performance flawlessly unfolding

in the Non-Physical realms.

It had 'already happened'!

All I had to do then

was to warm up my body

and allow it to happen once again,

this time in the Physical.

Try this process.

Find a quiet place, and allow your body to deeply relax.

Then 'look within' and watch the incredible details of what it is that you want to experience *as it unfolds in the Non-Physical.*

Continue to relax, noticing any communication from your Non-Physical Self as it guides you in what to do, not do, or how to be in the Physical.

And leave the rest up to the Non-Physical. What you have 'seen' and energetically felt will, in time, come to be experienced in the Physical. The Non-Physical will 'arrive' in the Physical, as it were.

Enjoy this process. It is powerful, magical, delightful, and as real as real gets!

The Non-Physical will 'arrive' in the Physical.

Enjoy this process. It is powerful,
magical, delightful –
and as real as real gets!

Simplexity - Summary So Far

Once we have clarified What We Want, it is vitally important that we recognize How We Feel.

Our feelings are a direct indicator of the direction in which our thoughts are focusing. In other words, they are a confirmation to us that we are Focusing Our Attention Upon our desires - rather than on their opposite.

Feeling good opens us to receiving.

Feeling other than good closes us down.

There are many powerful ways that we can direct how we feel - it isn't up to chance.

We can simply Decide. We can intentionally move to a better feeling using the 17 Levels of Consciousness as our 'map'. We can choose believable thoughts to generate good feelings, thus Getting On the Merry Go Round.

We can pay attention to our Inner Thinking and our Outer Thinking with an intention of bringing them into perfect alignment and harmony with each other.

We can practice How I Want to Feel Afterwards and Experiential Rehearsals to 'pre-pave the way' for our Physical reality to follow the beauty and bounty of our pre-rehearsed Non-Physical reality.

How We Feel is within our power *each and every moment.* We can *choose* How We Want to Feel, and in so doing, we actively set the stage for our desires to 'land'.

STEP 4

GET OUT OF THE WAY

It is the 'Vertical reality' which feeds and fuels

and fills us with inspiration.

The 'Horizontal reality'

simply interprets it and enjoys it.

L etting Your Non-Physical Self In

There comes a time in the creation of anything when we need to Get Out of The Way - we need to allow the Non-Physical its power to create.

John Randolph Price articulates brilliantly this process of attuning our focus from our fixation on the Physical to a gleeful awareness of our Non-Physical Self. In fact it is our Non-Physical Self that channels or flows into our Physical experience anything we desire which is not yet in our Physical experience. It has to come from the Non-Physical. This is 'Law'.

I highly recommend John's tiny yet extraordinary <u>The Abundance Book</u>.

To receive something new into our experience we must learn to let go the dominance of our functions of Thinking and Doing and attune more fully to our powerful functions of Visioning and Loving. It is our Visioner (King/Queen) and our Lover (Lover) who can create what does not yet exist. When we re-discover our true state of balance - our power to create - we shift our Thinker (Magician) and Doer (Warrior) into service to our Visioner and our Lover. This is the most powerful structure within us - the 'Horizontal reality' in service to the 'Vertical reality'.

For it is the 'Vertical reality' which feeds and fuels and fills us with inspiration. The 'Horizontal reality' simply interprets it and enjoys it.

As Marvin Anderson, a wonderful Unity Minister reminds us, the Physical is meant simply to bask in the Non-Physical. We are meant, in this Physical experience, to live in Joy.

Use the Meditation processes in Know What You Want to explore your Non-Physical reality and to shift your dominant perception from your Physical self to your Non-Physical Self.

This puts you in the 'seat' of your creator.

Resistance

We spoke earlier about doubt and how its presence can counter-act and ultimately negate the creation of our desires. It does this by causing 'friction' - or resistance - in our creative process.

In our workshops and private practice with many clients we have discovered three processes which are particularly effective in dissolving doubt and thus resistance.

They are 'Psychosomatic Energetics', 'Core Transformation' and 'The 12 Soul Powers'.

Psychosomatic Energetics

Psychosomatic Energetics (PSE) was developed in the late 20th century by two physicians and naturopaths in Germany. It recognizes that within us there are invisible 'energy blocks' which consume our life force and deter us from optimal vitality and well-being. These energy blocks arise from unresolved traumatic and/or chronic stress experiences and evidence themselves through what we know as 'symptoms' - disturbing thought patterns, destructive feeling patterns, and physical discomforts and diseases.

When these energy blocks dissolve, we regain vibrant health of body, heart and mind, naturally and effortlessly. Our patterns of coping (physical, mental and emotional) are no longer needed. Our 'masks' fall away, and we regain the joy and empowerment of our authentic self.

Colin and I are enthusiastically drawn to working with PSE as it is consistently effective, absolutely non-intrusive, respectful, and powerful in its results. The 'sources' of an individual's doubts and resistance dissolve simply through taking a course of compound homeopathic remedies which do the work, on a very deep level of the 'soul'.

When these energy blocks dissolve,

we regain vibrant health of body, heart and mind

naturally and effortlessly.

Our patterns of coping (physical, mental and emotional)

are no longer needed.

Our 'masks' fall away

and we regain the joy and empowerment

of our authentic self.

Working with PSE is a powerful way to assist people to plug in to their true power, positive outlook, and constructive, upward spiraling feelings - putting them in a place of leverage and great freedom to create the life they so clearly desire.

If this inspires you, contact us at info@veraxis.net.

It is important to realize
that all of our 'parts'
want our well-being.

Core Transformation

Core Transformation is a powerful process which was developed by Connirae and Tamara Andreas. These pioneering women recognized that our thoughts, beliefs and actions all arise from patterns deep in our subconscious mind.

It is important to realize that all of our 'parts' want our well-being. What happens in most of us is that aspects of our self become 'breached' - disoriented in their relationship to our well-being. This typically results from traumatic or chronic experiences of overwhelm, terror, or confusion.

When this happens, the inherent 'shock' causes parts of us to become twisted and 'snagged' inside of us - as if some move faster and some move slower and thus get 'caught'. Like when a baby becomes breached in relation to what would be the natural direction and flow of its birth.

Core Transformation is a gentle, powerful process in which we identify these breached - or resistant - aspects of ourselves and assist them respectfully to un-snag and align themselves in the direction of our desires and our ultimate well-being.

Which image 'feels' better to you?

or

If this inspires you, we occasionally offer workshops incorporating the Core Transformation process. And of course we'd be happy to guide you through this wonderful process in person or over the telephone. You can contact us at info@veraxis.net.

We also recommend the book Core Transformation by Connirae and Tamara Andreas.

The 12 Soul Powers

The 12 Soul Powers derives from Gnostic Christian teachings. It is a beautiful process which aligns all the aspects of our inner being - or 'soul' - in harmony with the creation of our desires.

In The 12 Soul Powers process we ...

1. Step into the Energy Field of **Love**, realizing that I Am Love

2. Declare our **Direction** by clarifying our desire

3. Stand behind our desire with our **Strength**

4. Engage our **Wisdom**, discerning what to do, not do, or be in support of the creation of our desire

5. Utilize the fuel of the **Power** of our words and thoughts

6. **Imagine** the experience of our fulfilled desire

7. Acknowledge our **Understanding** of our desire

8. Align our **Will** fully and completely with the creation of our desire

9. Coordinate **Order** in our Physical world to support the birth of our desire

The 12 Soul Powers effectively aligns our
'inner birth canal'.
It ensures that all aspects
of our inner being
are in harmony,
working *together* to fulfill our desires.

10. Fully enjoy our **Excitement** about our desire

11. **Renounce** anything which is in resistance to the manifestation of our desire

12. Recognize that we are **Life**, and thus are eternal and infinite

The 12 Soul Powers process effectively aligns our 'inner birth canal'. It ensures that all aspects of our inner being - our Non-Physical Self in relation to our Physical self - are in harmony and in co-creative relationship, working together to fulfill our desires.

If this process intrigues you, we frequently offer 12 Soul Powers based workshops. We also teach and guide individuals into using The 12 Soul Powers. Contact us at info@veraxis.net for more information.

You may also enjoy reading New Thoughts for a New Millennium edited by Michael Maday.

'The Beauty I See In You Is ... '

I first experienced 'The Beauty I See In You Is ... ' in a workshop presented by Peak Potentials. In a room of approximately two hundred people, a most magical experience evolved.

This is a radiantly joyful - and immediate - way to move out of resistance and into allowing. It connects us with what we love and value, re-setting our resonance to attract and receive What We Truly Want.

To explore this process on your own, simply look about you! And/or reflect in your inner mind. *Whatever* enters your awareness, begin the phrase 'The Beauty I See In You Is ... ' and - without thinking - complete the phrase.

Notice the next thing, person or place that arises in your awareness. Begin the phrase and - without thinking - complete it.

Continue this practice for a few minutes.

Then pause. Notice how you are feeling now! Are you still in resistance? How can you be?! When you are Focused on What You Want and *Love, this is What You Feel!*

You can use this practice when you 'need' to - that is, when you are aware that you are resisting your well-being, your desires.

However, I highly recommend that you use this practice *pro-actively* - and not just as a 'remedy' when you are aware that you are stuck.

Practice it daily - or even hourly. The more frequently you practice *recognizing what you appreciate,* the more you will attract things and experiences to you that you appreciate.

How does this work?

What you see and appreciate around you

awakens its likeness within you.

By noticing what you appreciate,

you shift your vibration

to **being what you like.**

As you become the nature of what you want,

it fluidly flows to you.

How does this work? What you see and appreciate around you awakens its likeness within you. By noticing what you appreciate, you shift your vibration from being what you don't like to **being what you like.** As you become the nature of what you want, it fluidly flows to you.

The fear factor could have sky-rocketed in me.

It didn't.

Because my Non-Physical Self guided me

with these words:

"Don't think too much."

<u>"Don't Think Too Much"</u>

I had just created a 'miracle' in completely healing a fractured kneecap. And I was onstage touring solo.

The 'buzz' was growing that my performance was a 'Must See', a 'Hot Show', 'Not to be missed'.

The fear factor could have sky-rocketed in me. It didn't. Because my Non-Physical Self guided me with these words: "Don't think too much."

When our mind becomes over-active, our thoughts either accelerate in the direction of excitement or of problem solving. Either way, over-active thoughts take us out of the 'now'.

With the support and guidance of my Non-Physical Self, I chanted to myself: "Don't think too much. Don't think too much. Don't think too much."

And in mere moments, all other thoughts disappeared.

I was left with the moment - the miraculous moment I was in. And free to enjoy it.

Do you ever notice yourself thinking yourself into fear, worry, or any other form of misery?

If you do, try this:

Silently (or audibly) repeat to yourself: "Don't think too much. Don't think too much. Don't think too much." … Until you begin to experience calm, the deepening of your breath, and the deliciousness of inner peacefulness.

For it is only when the mind is still (Magician) and unnecessary activity ceases (Warrior) that the 'runway' is open and clear for the true power of the Non-Physical (King/Queen and Lover) to be born.

Make space for your 'Vertical reality'.

"Don't think too much. Don't think too much. Don't think too much."

Enjoy your stillness.

Creative life is bliss.

You determine the content of your thoughts.

Become a master at *this* –

and you become a master

at creating whatever you want to have and experience.

'Stop' Button

Here is an easy and effective way to stop unwanted thoughts which would lead to unwanted feelings which would block and deter the creation of your desires.

Simply say to the thought: "Stop."

Imagine that you have a tape recorder with a Play and a Stop button.

When you realize that a thought is running through your brain 'without your permission', simply press Stop in your mind.

And the thought will disappear.

Try this.

Practice this.

It works.

With practice you will be able to *choose* which of the thoughts that arise in your brain you wish to think - and which of the thoughts that arise in your brain you wish to not think. *You* determine the nature and the content of your thoughts. Become a master at *this* - and you become a master at creating whatever you want to have and experience.

'Shred It'

I was in a private session with a client with a particularly strong 'runaway brain' when this process intuitively came to me.

Do you have a paper shredder? If not, get one.

Whenever you notice yourself thinking a thought which doesn't feel good, write it down. Then Shred It. Shred the thought by putting the piece of paper through the shredder.

This will physicalize your experience of *your* power to choose *your* thoughts.

You will then be able to do this anywhere, in your own mind, wherever you are. In other words, you will no longer need the paper shredder *in the Physical* to powerfully and effectively shred your unwanted thoughts.

Here's how it works:

Notice when you are thinking a thought which is in any way dis-empowering to you. You can identify dis-empowering thoughts by the way you *feel*. If a thought affects you by dragging you down, it is a dis-empowering thought. If it affects you by inspiring and energizing you, it is an empowering thought.

As soon as you notice that you are thinking a dis-empowering thought, 'Shred It'. In your imagination, put it through your 'shredder'. Just as if you were to write it down and put it through your Physical paper shredder, put it etherically through your Non-Physical shredder.

And notice what happens.

It is immediately gone! Vanished!

… And there in the void is the beautiful vacancy - the emptiness which follows. Where there would have been a runaway train of thoughts, there is … delicious, silent stillness.

Practice this. Try it out a few times to gain your confidence in it. Discover that *it works each and every time. It is so easy.*

You can apply this process with dis-empowering feelings, too.

As soon as you become aware that you are feeling a feeling which is not one of joy, love, and peace, 'Shred It'.

Just like you did with your unwanted thoughts - immediately shred your unwanted feelings.

This creates an immediate relief. And, as the Philosopher J. Krishnamurti described so eloquently, this creates a 'gap' - a new space in which a new response can arise. Shredding an unwanted thought or feeling effectively creates an opening - a clearing - just like the impeccably quiet stillness after a storm. It interrupts the habitual pattern of the mind. It allows new Light to enter in.

When you discover that this or any practice works for you, share it! Share it with your friends, your family, your associates. The more we free ourselves into good feeling feelings and good feeling thoughts *that we believe,* the more we are a channel through which Love flows into the Earth and the human experience.

And there in the void

is the beautiful vacancy – the emptiness which follows.

Where there would have been

a runaway train of thoughts,

there is ... delicious, silent stillness.

This benefits us all.

When you discover a practice that works for you, share it!

The more we free ourselves into good feelings

and good feeling thoughts *that we believe,*

the more we are a channel through which Love flows

into the Earth and the human experience.

This benefits us all.

Know It Will Come

As a child, before you experienced any sort of trauma (if this was a part of your life story), you likely Knew That It Will Come. You sensed, accurately and excitedly inside of you, when something you desired and anticipated was about to arrive.

In your innocence of knowing that the universe is benevolent and good, you Knew That What You Wanted Would Come.

You 'just knew it'.

There was no doubt.

Thus there was no resistance.

You opened to your natural abundance.

And you allowed yourself to receive.

This natural state of Knowing likely began to diminish and wane when adults around you, conditioned in a similar way when they were children, began to suggest to you that you cannot have what you want. That you have to settle for what you have. That you have to be content with what you've got. That to want something that you don't have is to be selfish, greedy, expectant, and demanding.

They only taught you this because this was what they were taught by other 'innocent people'. Innocence and naivety simply mean 'not yet aware'.

They were not yet aware.

What were they not aware of?

They were not aware that *there is no such thing as scarcity.*

They mis-understood, like so many others before them, believing that to want something means that it must arise in the Physical. That it must come 'from' the Physical. That there must be an *evidence of supply of it - in the Physical.*

They weren't aware yet (they had 'forgotten'), that there is always an abundance of supply. This abundance - this 'overflowing bathtub' - is in the Non-Physical. We must simply learn (meaning to remember) how to tap in to it.

And so here you are - an awakening adult, wanting more of something which you are beginning to realize that you value.

Know That It Will Come.

Want it.

Give Your Attention To It.

Notice How You Feel, guiding your feelings into states of better and better feelings.

And Get Out of The Way.

It *will* come.

Know it, from the depth of your being. This Knowing is you connecting with your Non-Physical Self.

For everything that you want exists *in the Non-Physical.* Open your tap to receive it.

Knowing is your tap.

<u>Adjusting Your Thermostat</u>

Just like a thermostat determines the air temperature in a room, our inner thermostat determines the 'set point' of our experience.

We set a thermostat to regulate our experience of *comfort,* yes?

And we have already discussed that - in order to receive into the Physical something which we don't yet have - we must expand beyond our current *comfort* zone, yes?

Within you, invisible to you, you have 'set' your thermostat for every category of your experience - your degree of satisfaction in relationships, your degree of success in your career and finances, your degree of courage and willingness to explore new horizons, your degree of health and well-being. What you have set is what you are familiar with.

If you want something in your Physical experience that you don't yet have, you can be sure that your 'inner thermostat' is set to *what you currently have!*

Just like a thermostat

determines the air temperature in a room,

your 'inner thermostat'

determines the 'set point' of your experience.

So **re-set your thermostat** to the 'temperature' of What You Want.

Imagine that you have a dial within you. Place your fingers on the dial ... and move it up one degree. Go about your day. Acclimatize to this *new inner set point.*

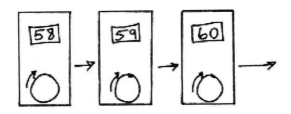

At the same time tomorrow, take a quiet moment and envision your dial within you. Place your fingers upon it ... and move it up one degree (or more if you feel ready to!). Go about your day. Acclimatize to this *new inner set point.*

Do this until you feel - deep within yourself in a way that is fully believable to you - that you are now at the 'temperature' of

What You Want. In other words, you are now *at the same vibration as it.*

You have a thermostat within you for every key area of your life. Explore raising your dial in one area at a time or several simultaneously. The Law of Critical Mass will work in your favor, as the shifting of one inner thermostat will support the re-setting of the next.

Enjoy your new 'temperature'. Enjoy the *new you!*

Let Go (Non-Attachment to the Outcome)

When we realize that our Non-Physical Self has a vastness of vantage that 'we' - our Physical self - do not have, then we can more easily realize that our Non-Physical Self is tapped in to resources and pathways that we cannot 'see'.

There comes a time - precisely after steps one, two, and three - when we must move on to step four: Let Go. Get Out of The Way.

We must recognize and accept that 'we' cannot create that which is not yet Physical - without the incredible aid of our Non-Physical Self and all that it has connection to.

Let go.

Let go to your Non-Physical Self.

Let go of the reins.

Let go of the reins …

Let your Non-Physical Self do the rest.

Allow yourself to be surprised – and delighted – by the
beauty and the bounty of what It gives to you.

Let Go.

And trust.

One of the most lucid, comprehensible ways to do this is to *let go of your attachment to and assumptions of how, when, and in what form your desire will appear.*

Your Non-Physical Self, from its incredible "Birds' Eye View" perspective, knows far more than 'you' do of what is ideal for you.

You can only know what you want from your angle of perception which is based upon your past experiences, what you've learned or heard or read from others, and the clarity you have gained in the now based upon the contrast of your past experiences.

Your Non-Physical Self can 'see' so much more than this.

So take your hands off the wheel.

Once you've established and declared What You Want; you've given Your Focused Attention To It (and taken it off of what you don't want); you've learned to recognize How You Feel as a signal of whether you are moving in the direction of, or away from, what you desire and thus you are actively moving yourself into better feeling thoughts; then it is time to Let Go.

Let Your Non-Physical Self do the rest. Let *It* determine what ingredients to draw together, where to find them, and how to present them to you in a way that will most comprehensively fulfill your desire.

Allow It to present you with your requested gift.

Allow yourself to be surprised - and delighted. And perhaps even overwhelmed by the beauty and bounty of what It gives to you.

Let Go.

And trust.

We all –

no matter how distressed we may be at times –

have the resources we need *within us*

to respond constructively in any situation.

'Moving Hands'

Milton Erickson was a pioneer in hypnotherapy and recognizing that we all - no matter how distressed we may be at times - have the resources we need *within us* to respond constructively in any situation.

'Moving Hands' is a powerful Tool to access - easily - our masterful inner resources.

Sit comfortably[1] in a place where you will be undisturbed for an hour. This process may take a few minutes - it may take some time.

---

[1] As 'Moving Hands' is a conscious hypnosis process, it is advised to allow several hours following its practice for stillness and integration. If you will be driving or operating machinery of any sort following its practice, be sure to take sufficient time to re-establish a clear state of awareness of your physical environment. If you have any questions or wish personal assistance in exploring this practice, please contact info@veraxis.net.

Hold your hands in front of you, palms facing each other, at shoulder height, approximately one foot apart.

As you allow your arms to be gently suspended, airborne, articulate in a few simple words what it is that you are seeking a clear answer or resolution to. This is what you will be turning over to your *unconscious mind.*

Once you have articulated, in a few words, the question to which you are seeking resolution or the outcome that you desire, simply breathe.

You will begin to notice - quite quickly or very gradually (this varies with each person and each time you engage 'Moving Hands') - that your hands are beginning to move toward each other ... *involuntarily.* That is, 'you' are not moving your hands!

Stay with this. Simply relax and breathe, as your hands continue *their* journey toward each other.

When your hands arrive at the point where they would cross, one will naturally fold beneath the other toward your lap. They will continue their arc of motion until both hands are resting on your lap.

Sometime within this process
downward, as if it is nodding to 'sleep'.
alert.

Shortly after your hands have landed at rest on y
your head has dropped forward, you will feel refreshed -
waking from a deep and very restful sleep.

There is nothing more to 'do' now. You have done the
Practice. Go about your day.

Sometime in the near future you will begin to notice -
effortlessly - the arising of your clarity. For your 'unconscious mind'
will have sorted through its files and accessed the necessary
information to deliver to you - on a conscious level - that which you
asked it for.

'Moving Hands' is a direct bridge between the conscious and
the unconscious minds.

ify: The 'doing' of this practice is merely the sitting in
e, the positioning of the hands with palms towards each
out a foot apart, and the articulating in a few simple words
it is that you are seeking in terms of clarity or resolution.

The rest of this practice takes care of itself. There is no need for you to follow the notes above. They are not 'directions'. They are simply a description of what you will experience, in your own way.

It is the unconscious mind that moves the hands and ultimately the head - as if to say to you, the 'conscious' person, 'I am taking care of your request'. The moving of your hands and head is a signal from your inner Self to your outer self that your request has been heard and its response is underway.

Turn It Over To Gestation

We are a part of nature. We humans tend often to forget this.

And as a part of nature, we are subject to the incredible stages in the process of creation.

A seed is planted.
It gestates for awhile.

Nutrients feed it.
It begins to sprout.

More nutrients feed it.
It begins to grow.

More nutrients feed it.
It grows strong and clear.

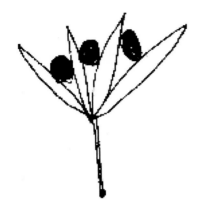

More nutrients feed it.
It reaches its peak, its
'full potential'.

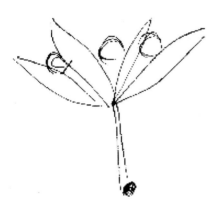

More nutrients feed it.
It transitions beyond
'form', expanding
infinitely, eternally.

This is the process of any creation. Some perceive transition beyond form as 'death'. It is simply a transition from the Physical into the Non-Physical, again.

When you clarify and you declare What You Want, you are planting a seed.

When you Focus Your Attention Upon It - purely and intently (rather than on its opposite - what you don't want), you are feeding it nutrients.

When You Feel Good, you have your first evidence in the Physical that the creation of your desire is underway. It has begun to 'sprout in you'.

And so you naturally, excitedly feed it more nutrients.

And it grows more. And you feel good. And you feed it more attention - more *belief.* More faith. More trust. You begin to energetically open to its birth. You prepare to welcome it.

And then it begins to appear in your Physical experience in ways even more magical than your feeling incredibly good.

And you feed it more of your excited, appreciative attention.

And it grows stronger.

And stronger.

And stronger.

When you clarify a desire,

you are planting a seed.

When you feel good,

you have your first evidence in the Physical

that the creation of your desire is underway.

It begins to 'sprout in you'.

There is a phase, in the creation of anything, when the seed gestates. The seed is 'invisible' during this phase of time. It is growing. It is preparing for its birth. And yet it is not visible, tangible - 'Physical' - yet.

Understanding this gives us enormous ease, relief, faith and trust in relation to the birth process. It is like an expectant father, waiting outside the delivery room.

There is a period of time when we must 'wait'.

There is a phase in the creation of anything
when the seed gestates.
The seed is 'invisible' during this phase of time.
It is growing. It is preparing for its birth.
And yet it is not yet 'Physical'.

The most expedient way to create anything is this:

1. **Clarify What You Want** - and Declare It

2. **Focus Your Attention Upon It** - being mindful to 'de-invest' your attention from its opposite - what you don't want

3. Ascertain that you are moving in the direction of creating it - **Be Aware of How You Feel**. (If you notice other than good feelings, choose a better feeling thought(s) until you are feeling good.)

4. Then surrender it to 'invisibility' - turn it over to the gestation process - **Get Out of The Way**

When you do this, something remarkable will occur.

Some time later, when you may even have forgotten the intensity of your desire, it will appear. It will be complete, fully dressed, absolutely whole. There will be no 'work' for you to do.

You will have allowed the natural process of gestation to do the work.

Try this with anything you desire - anything you wish to have or have more of in your life.

Do the four steps above.

And enjoy the harvest that begins to spill in.

Accept What Is, En-Joy, and Be Patient

A few weeks before writing this, I experienced a difficult day. I meditated, as I typically do when I encounter anything which is not clearly flowing.

And this message came to me:

"Accept What Is. En-Joy - Be in Joy with Everything That Is. And Be Patient."

Take a deep breath.

And reflect on these words, slowly, for yourself.

Drink in the meaning that they carry and which they generously deliver to *you*.

Accept What Is.

Be In Joy.

And Be Patient.

The Non-Physical realm is timeless, omni-dimensional, limitless consciousness. Your thinking brain is wired into time.

To enjoy the creative process, it is helpful to become aware and accepting of the non-linear nature of creation.

The baby will be born when the baby is born.

Practice Smiling

Thich Nhat Hanh, a brilliant and compassionate Vietnamese Buddhist monk, reminds us so simply and eloquently why we must practice smiling.

When we smile, our muscles relax.

When we smile, our heart opens.

When we smile, we forget our worries.

When we smile, we remember that
we are part of a bigger story.

When we smile, we feel love flowing effortlessly and generously throughout our being.

When we smile, we feel good.

When we smile, we create a ripple effect of love around us.

When we smile, we bring Light and Love into this world.

When we smile, we become peace.

When we smile, we model peace.

When we smile, others around us are affected by our peace.

When we smile, they become happy too.

There is tremendous generosity in smiling.

And it is 'free'. It doesn't cost us anything. In fact, it gives to everyone it touches.

What does smiling have to do with receiving what we want?

When we smile, we have automatically let go of resistance.

And when we are no longer resisting *anything,* we are completely open to receiving anything and everything that we desire.

There is tremendous generosity in smiling.

And it is 'free'. It doesn't cost us anything.

In fact,

it gives to everyone it touches.

So practice smiling. For ten minutes a day, focus your attention upon smiling.

At first it may seem unnatural, as if you are trying to do something contrary to how you are actually feeling.

Guess what! Smiling will *change* the way you feel. Smile for even just thirty seconds and you will notice a remarkable lifting in the way you feel. 'Check' yourself using Hawkins' 17 Level "Map of Consciousness" or Abraham's "Emotional Guidance System". Where are you now on the upwardly spiraling scale of good feelings?

The better you feel, the more open you are to receive.

So practice smiling for ten minutes every day. If you feel drawn to, write a note in your journal to witness how you feel before your practice - and write another note in your journal *after* your ten minutes of smiling practice. How has it changed you? Who have you become?

Practicing smiling can be one of the biggest and most precious gifts you ever give to yourself.

And in giving it to yourself, you are giving it to everyone.

Self Acceptance

I had an 'aha' last evening while practicing yoga: If I am fully Self accepting, I am fully allowing.

In other words, Self acceptance and resistance can't co-exist. Once I am fully *Self* accepting, I am fully and completely in a state of allowing - open to receive.

For there is only one thing that we can really resist, and that is our Self. Our resistance of any 'thing' is merely an outer ripple of our inner self-rejection.

Self-rejection arises out of experiences of wounding, large and small. We are also taught in our modern culture to reject our Self - so that we can perceive a need for products 'outside' of us. This is a major element in our current economy.

Self acceptance is simple. Once we accept our Selves, our lives become very simple. We no longer perceive a 'need' for anything. We are no longer dependent on that which is 'outside' of us.

When I am fully Self accepting,
I am fully allowing myself to receive.

This is an enormous shift for most of us.

Once we make this shift (and *as* we make it, for it is a process), we fully and truly realize that the Source of our good - of everything we need and desire - already exists *inside of us.*

And in being Self accepting, we are naturally in a state of openness *to our Selves.*

Do you see it? Can you catch this one? **When you accept your Self, you accept your Source. Your receiving channel is completely open.** There is nothing in the way to receiving anything and everything you want.

How do we practice Self acceptance?

One of the best ways I know is to lie in bed for a few moments in the morning before getting up. Say to yourself: "I love you _____ (your full name)."

Say this until you feel the love traveling toward you, 'through' you, from you. It's like sending a gift to yourself *and then receiving it!*

Practice this every morning. And notice what begins to change in the way you relate to yourself and treat yourself.

Another way to practice Self acceptance is to notice when you are in resistance to something - when you feel bitter, resentful or jealous; when you are pushing away something that you really want; when you feel irritable; when you feel sad, angry or depressed; when your energy is low.

As soon as you notice any of these 'signals of resistance', stop. Go to Hawkins' 17 Level "Map of Consciousness" or Abraham's "Emotional Guidance System". Recognize where you are *in this moment* on that scale. Decide where you want to be. And move yourself in that direction - by choosing a better feeling thought.

As you begin to move upwards - spiraling up in your feelings - you will naturally begin to resist less and open more to your true desires.

Another great tool for this is 'Core Transformation'. You can learn the basics of it from the book of the same name, or we can be your expert guides and lead you through it in a Coaching session - in person or via telephone.

The point is, 'un-breach' yourself. Disentangle the contradictory knots inside of you. Get yourself heading in the direction of your upwardly spiraling good feelings ... *in the direction of your Self.*

Just like an eagle circling upwards toward the sun, free yourself of resistance and *fly.*

There is only one thing that we can really resist –

and that is our Self.

Our resistance of any 'thing'

is merely an outer ripple

of our inner self-rejection.

Love yourself. Accept your Self.

And all good things will flow unto you.

Simplexity - Summary So Far

Once we have clarified What We Want and have consistently monitored How We Feel to confirm that Our Attention Is Upon It, we must Let Go. We must Get Out of The Way.

This is akin to a mother allowing her cervix to open so that the baby can be born.

When we are over-active in 'doing' and 'thinking' we tend to meddle with the powers of creation. We 'get in their way'.

When we are aligned with our 'Vertical reality' of 'Visioning' and 'Loving' we are "Letting Go … and Letting God". We are allowing the magnificent wisdom of the creative process to be at play within us.

Getting Out of The Way is dissolving our resistance to receiving our own good. It is the process of Letting Our Non-Physical Self In.

Psychosomatic Energetics, Core Transformation, and The 12 Soul Powers are valuable tools and processes to assist us in this vital step to receiving our desires.

"Don't Think Too Much", the 'Stop' Button, and 'Shred It' are powerful practices for quieting the runaway brain ... creating still space on our runway for our gifts to land.

Knowing It Will Come is a commitment of faith that this process works - each and every time. Why not ease our journey? Why not save ourselves the misery of doubt?!?

Letting Go (Non-Attachment to the Outcome) - of our fixation on the 'idea' of precisely what our desire will appear as in the Physical and how and when it will arrive - brings tremendous peace and joy, increasing our positive anticipation as we await the arrival of What We Want.

Turning It Over To Gestation respects the creative process of *nature* which is present every time something is wanted and received.

Accepting What Is, En-Joying it, and Being Patient take pressure off of the creative process, bringing us into the beauty and appreciation of the present moment.

Practicing Smiling immediately releases resistance and opens us to receive, as does Self Acceptance.

When we accept our Self, all good can - and will - come to us.

Read this book over and over again, until you 'get it'.

Until you understand –

which means to 'stand under' –

to have an 'aha' recognition of –

how abundance works.

Becoming A Master Creator

Master Creator has developed these:

1.   Understanding

2.   Tools

3.   Practice

4.   Consistent and Reliable Results

<u>Understanding</u>

Understanding comes from exposure to new ideas. Sometimes we need to encounter new ideas from several angles.

Read this book over and over again, until you 'get it'. Until you understand - which means to 'stand under', to have an 'aha' recognition - of how abundance works.

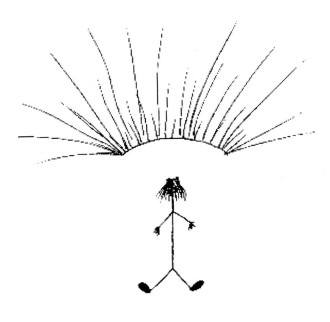

Do these things.

Do them often.

And you will change the energy field

in which you exist.

Simply put, you will open

your energy pores to attraction.

You will refine your selection.

And you will allow yourself to receive.

To understand - to stand under - is a humbling experience of being awed by an awareness greater than anything we had ever contemplated before.

Read any other books that you find yourself drawn to on the topics of abundance, personal healing, and 'waking up'. Read them over and over again until you experience 'ahas'.

Watch DVDs and listen to CDs which teach and expound on these principles. Do so over and over again until you experience 'ahas'.

Connect with and spend your precious time with people who are also exploring these ideas. Talk openly with them about how your thinking is changing, how your mind is opening, how you are doing and being and behaving differently. Ask them how they are approaching this new learning. Share 'tips' with each other. *Share your 'ahas'.*

And above all, meditate with your Self - communicate with your Non-Physical Self, your genius guide who Knows abundance and its 'how to' process inside out. Allow your Non-Physical Self to be your intimate, trusted Teacher. Your very revered friend.

Do these things.

Do them often.

And you will change the energy field in which you exist. You will shift out of a lower vibration experience of life into a higher vibration experience of life.

Simply put, you will open your energy pores to attraction. You will refine your selection. And you will allow yourself to receive.

Tools

Gather your tools.

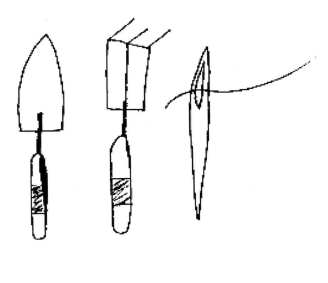

Use the practices in this book. And those in other books, DVDs, and CDs that you find yourself drawn to. Explore tools that others in your expanding circle of friends share with you.

Try them on.

See if they work!

If they seem to not work, do an honest inner inquiry.

Is there a grain of doubt that is obscuring your trust or your desire?

If there is, use the tools in this book and others that you discover to 'un-breach' this doubt. In so doing you will harness its un-breached energy as your friend and greatest ally.

Practice

Use your tools.

Tools are worthless in a dusty, dark shed.

Bring them 'into the light'. Bring them into your active experience, each and every day.

Choose the tools that feel most natural to you.

When will you practice them?

How will you remind yourself to practice?

Like any athlete or great musician you become great - proficient, masterful, with consistent and reliable results - *by practicing.*

Would you expect to play Rachmaninoff's Piano Concerto No. 3 without any practice? Or beat Tiger Woods in a round of golf?

Practice of valuable tools,

with understanding,

is the key.

How can you expect to experience results of abundance in your life without practice?

Practice of valuable Tools, with Understanding, *is the key.*

Consistent and Reliable Results

Imagine yourself, a few weeks from now, having diligently and consistently applied your understanding through the practice of the tools you've chosen ...

How do you look?

How do you feel?

Listen to the tone and timbre of your voice. What are you saying?

Who are you with?

Where are you?

What is with you?

What has changed since your 'now'?

This is the magic of abundance: When you begin to Understand - to 'get it' - the Simplicity of Abundance; and you gather some Tools that you feel drawn to and like; and you Practice them ... the Magic begins.

You begin to realize ... that *you* have created your desire in co-creation with your Non-Physical Self - using the Understanding, Tools, and Practice that *you* have committed to.

You are the reason for your results.

This is the freedom spoken of by sages throughout the ages in every spiritual tradition of the world.

Learn how to create through the powers within you and you are free.

You are the reason for your results.

This is the freedom
spoken of by sages
throughout the ages
in every spiritual tradition of the world.

Learn how to create
through the powers within you
and you are free.

The Amazing Alchemy of Transformation

You cannot get there from here.

You must go through to arrive.

In other words, you cannot simply Want and Receive without *transforming*. Any beliefs, patterns of thought, speech and behavior, or any other kind of ruttedness that has held you in 'lack' *in any area of your life* will shift in the process of Mastering the Laws of Creation.

You will become a 'new', more vibrant, much more confident, more relaxed, appreciative, respectful human being.

Because this is the path.

This is the Alchemical Path. Of Creation.

You must rise to the level of consciousness of the Creative Mind.

You will become a 'new', vibrant,

much more confident, relaxed, appreciative,

respectful human being.

Because this is the path.

This is the Alchemical Path.

Of Creation.

Anyone can do this. You are not exempt. Regardless of upbringing, family social class, apparent intelligence, and whatever programs and patterns you have developed throughout the years, with truly determined, heart-felt application of these Principles, you too can - and will - succeed.

Practice is how you amass the rocket fuel to blast yourself up - and out - of the downward spiral of 'lack' that has brought you to this book.

Understanding.

Tools.

Practice.

Success.

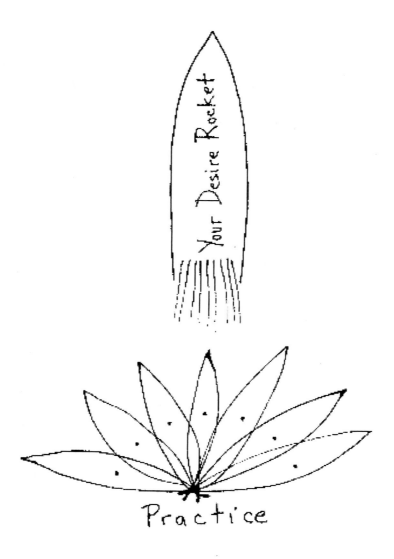

Simplexity - Summary So Far

There are four steps to becoming a Master Creator. They are ...

- Understanding
- Tools
- Practice
- Consistent and Reliable Results

When we embark on the journey of Knowing What We Want, Focusing Our Attention Upon It, Becoming Aware of How We Feel, and Getting Out of The Way, we become part of The Amazing Alchemy of Transformation.

To get something we don't already have, we must open ourselves to expand beyond our current comfort zone. We must release our resistance to receiving it. We must allow our own good.

This, inherently, begins a process of our own awakening to our Non-Physical Self, our inherent good-ness, and our infinite capacity for Love.

The path of learning how to get what we want is a course of Self-discovery.

In the innocence of our desires, we set forth a rocket to 'God'. The message in our rocket is this: "Make me whole. Give me all that I desire. Make me happy. Give me what I want."

Our innocence leads to our mature awakening as we realize, little by little, that we always have been whole. That we always have been abundant. That this 'seed of Source is within us'. It has been all along.

The process of learning how to get What We Want thus becomes a recognition that there is no lack. And so we set about to remove the barricades to our own good. Through the '4 Steps to Plenty' we remove those barricades. And as we learn this once, we repeat this over and over again, creating the Consistent and Reliable Results of a Master Creator.

When what we innocently thought we wanted was 'love' or 'money' or 'health', what we get is the powerful Tools to Create What We Want, each and every time.

Welcome to the world of Master Creators. With Practice of the '4 Steps to Plenty' you will soon be one.

CELEBRATING YOUR SUCCESSES

Anyone can do this. You are not exempt.

T here is a powerful Law of the Universe that will aid you magnificently in propelling you forward: *That Which Is Given Attention Grows.*

And so Celebrate Your Successes.

When you recognize your Successes - 'large' and 'small' - you are sending out a gratitude message which says: "I like this. I love this. I would love to have more of this."

And the universe responds.

So be sure - sure to Notice Your Successes. And Celebrate Them!

Here are a few ways. Be creative. I'm sure you'll come up with many, many more.

There is a powerful Law of the Universe
that will aid you magnificently
in propelling you forward:
That Which Is Given Attention Grows.
And so Celebrate Your Successes.

Creation Log

Creation successes come in all shapes and sizes. Some appear so 'small' that we easily overlook them. The more *sensitive* we are - attuned to the creation process which we are actively in - the more of the *subtle* signals of success we will begin to notice.

Simply put, we will notice the *feelings* of creation. And Celebrate them.

We will notice the *sprouting* of creation. And Celebrate this.

We will notice the *budding* of creation. And Celebrate this.

We will notice the plant bursting forth from the soil. And we will continue to Celebrate.

In other words, Celebrate every tiny stage of creation that you notice. Even if it is a fleeting instant of 'yahoo!' Celebrate it.

Send a message to the universe, consistently and powerfully, that you are receiving - with graciousness and gratitude in your heart - what it is bringing into your life.

One way to do this, easily and effortlessly, is to have a Creation Log. You can purchase or make a separate journal for this. Or designate a column in your day-timer.

Every time you notice something 'new' arising in your experience as a result of your declaration of desire, write it down.

At the end of the day, review this list and notice how much evidence there has been *today* of your creation coming into Physical fruition.

The value of a Creation Log is this: Every time you realize that your creation is underway, *You Focus More Of Your Attention Upon It.* You pivot more and more clearly and powerfully away from what you don't want and into what you *do.* Like a huge ship turning direction in the sea. By recognizing and acknowledging your Successes in Creation, you are turning your ship powerfully in the direction of What You Want.

Yes! Yes! Yes!

Every time you notice even a glimmer of evidence that what you want is beginning to appear in your Physical reality, stop right where you are. Raise your hands and face to the sky. And rejoice, "Yes! Yes! Yes!"

If you are too shy to do this (initially!), or you're in a meeting at the precise moment when your recognition of your success dawns upon you, or you need to keep your hands on your bicycle handlebars or your steering wheel, then turn your *energy* upwards. And silently, with a voice of glee, say "Yes! Yes! Yes!"

Then notice how you feel.

Appreciation is a key. Gratitude - and Self-recognition of our diligence towards something We Truly Want - feels great!

And great feelings move us swiftly in the direction of our creation.

"Yes! Yes! Yes!"

There are so many ways to Celebrate!

My List of Ways To Celebrate

There are so many ways to Celebrate. Some cost money, some don't. Some require time, some don't. Some are best done with friends, some are best done alone. Some are internal. Some are external.

Make a list, right here, right now, of some of the ways that *you* can Celebrate.

Ways that I *do* Celebrate

❖

❖

❖

❖

Ways that I *could* Celebrate

❖

❖

❖

❖

Ways that I *will* Celebrate

❖

❖

❖

❖

Congratulations! You're on your way!

Milestones

Milestones are significant turning points.

How will you know when you're truly aligned with your Simplicity of Abundance?

How will you know when you've released any old resistance, and your creation of a desire is underway?

How will you know when you're becoming a Master Creator, able to create *at will* your desires?

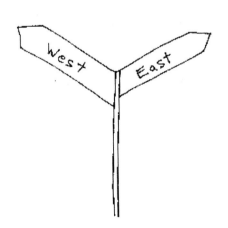

How will you know when it's time to share what you've learned with other people, assisting them to free themselves from the illusion of lack - into the truth of plenty?

How will you know when you're applying your Mastery in the highest possible ways that you can?

How will you acknowledge your Milestones of Success and Personal Growth?

Ancient alchemists spoke of 'turning lead into gold'.

How will you recognize your *Milestones?*

And how will you Celebrate them?

Start your list of ideas right here ...

❖

❖

❖

❖

Creating a Ceremony of Gratitude

There are many ways to Celebrate and express our Gratitude. Creating a Ceremony slows us down from the pace of our daily living. It Focuses Our Attention with laser stillness on the sacredness of the *now*.

A Ceremony can be informal and spontaneous – or pre-planned with precision and detail.

The point is to take open-ended time to Celebrate and give your pure attention to that which you are Grateful for.

A Ceremony of Gratitude could be …

- Lighting a candle and reflecting on your Success as you gaze into the flame

- Arranging a bouquet of flowers which represent your Joy in your accomplishment

- Creating a sacred space, demarcated with stones or leaves or crystals or … and stepping into the space to

Be imaginative.

Step outside of your comfort zone.

A Celebration is worth stretching for!

reflect on and experience your Gratitude for what you have achieved

- Inviting friends to read a poem with you or watch a sunset to commemorate your Creative Success

- Taking a slow, contemplative walk (Walking Meditation) in a forest, being mindful of your Gratitude for how you have allowed the Non-Physical to appear in your Physical experience

Be imaginative.   Step outside of your comfort zone.   A Celebration is worth stretching for!

What are some of the elements that you might incorporate into your Ceremony of Gratitude?

❖

❖

❖

❖

A Ceremony is a sacred time of reflection. Take slow, quiet, deep breaths. Move with grace and mindfulness. Notice the details of your inner experience. And above all – En-Joy!

Simplexity - Summary So Far

Celebrating Our Successes is how we say to the universe that we like what we are getting and we want more! More love, health, finances, leisure time - whatever it is that we are asking for and creating.

The universe responds to our joy. It wants to give us more of what makes us happy.

A Creation Log assists us to notice our Successes in becoming a Master Creator.

Saying Yes! Yes! Yes! affirms to us that we are doing well. *And* it simultaneously thanks our Non-Physical Self and acknowledges that we like what we are receiving. It is like saying 'Thank You' when we receive a present. The giver feels appreciated, and the channels are thus open for them to give again, and again, and again.

Recognizing our Milestones is a powerful way to acknowledge our Mastery and our Successes.

There are so many potential ways to Celebrate. Creating our own personal Ceremony of Gratitude is a wonderful way to do so.

Have fun! The more you take time and attention to Celebrate Your Successes, the more quickly you will propel yourself forward into the realm of Allowing All That You Desire.

True happiness arises from a sense of belonging –

a recognition that we are a part

of a great whole.

ETHICAL ABUNDANCE

Spirit is eternal and ephemeral.

The more we evolve to desiring that which is –

in its essence –

an expression of spirit,

the less we are drawn

to a surplus of material things.

Creating with Consciousness

True happiness arises from a sense of belonging - a recognition that we are a part of a great whole.

As we become Master Creators we naturally evolve consciously, becoming oriented towards the well-being of this whole.

There is so much wealth available to us which is not material - abundant health, friendships, love, time in nature, Self-love, music and the arts - to name a few. All of these arise from renewable resources. They are expressions of *spirit*.

Spirit is eternal and ephemeral. The more we evolve to desiring that which is, in its essence, an expression of spirit, the less we are drawn to a surplus of material things.

It is a matter of balance.

There is so much wealth available to us

which is not material –

abundant health, friendships, love, time in nature,

Self-love, music and the arts –

to name a few.

All of these arise from renewable resources.

They are expressions of *spirit.*

Your Ecological Footprint

Each of us has an 'ecological footprint' - a degree to which we impact the well-being of the Earth. Our Footprint includes our use of natural resources and our contribution to pollution.

Giving feels great. Being generous feels wonderful.
It lifts us up – literally.

Open yourself to receiving plenty – unabashedly –
and giving away plenty – equally unabashedly.

Become an ecologically and socially aware
'clearing house' for wealth.

The more we are aware of our yearning for *spirit* - and thus the more we allow our wanting to fulfill us from the inside out - the less we impact the Earth with our Footprint.

Be aware of your desires for things material. *It is a matter of balance.* Become aware of where and by whom they are made, with what materials, and by what processes. Often there are many options or 'models' of material things. Choose from those which are ethically responsible.

Social Awareness

We can have so much and give so much.

Again, the more we become aware of our primary yearning for *spirit,* the more we open ourselves to receiving plenty. And thus the more we begin to experience surplus - an overflowing fountain - a state of having more than we need.

Giving feels great. Being generous feels wonderful. It lifts us up - literally.

Open yourself to receiving plenty - unabashedly - and giving away plenty - equally unabashedly.

Become an ecologically and socially aware 'clearing house' for wealth.

There is so much wealth on this beautiful planet, and so much more available to us. Use the Understanding, Tools, and Practices presented in this book to take your feet off your brakes. Allow yourself the pristine birthright of being truly abundant. Model the 'how' of this to others around you, like a ripple in a pond. And give away.

Give away, knowing that your Mastery of Creation will always give you more.

Give away ... because we are all a part of a greater whole. We are symbiotically inter-connected. Ultimately, our thrival and its are inextricably linked.

And give away ... simply because *giving feels great.*

Give away,

knowing that your Mastery of Creation

will always give you more.

QUESTIONS AND RESPONSES

P lease feel free to submit your Questions to info@veraxis.net. Select Questions and their Responses will be included in the next Edition of <u>The Simplexity of Abundance – 4 Steps to Plenty</u>.

Thank You!

Afterword

It has been a delight writing this book. Thank you for this opportunity to share my practices and wisdom with you.

For more information on who we are and what we do, please visit us at www.HeartSongSolutions.ca and www.veraxis.net.

It will be a pleasure to connect with you more directly, to hear your Success Stories, and to receive your Questions as you delve deeply into your quest for Abundance.

May you experience Abundance in *all* areas of your life - Health, Relationships, Career, Finances, Friendships, Personal Growth and Fun.

☺ Ariole

Vancouver, Canada

February 24, 2007

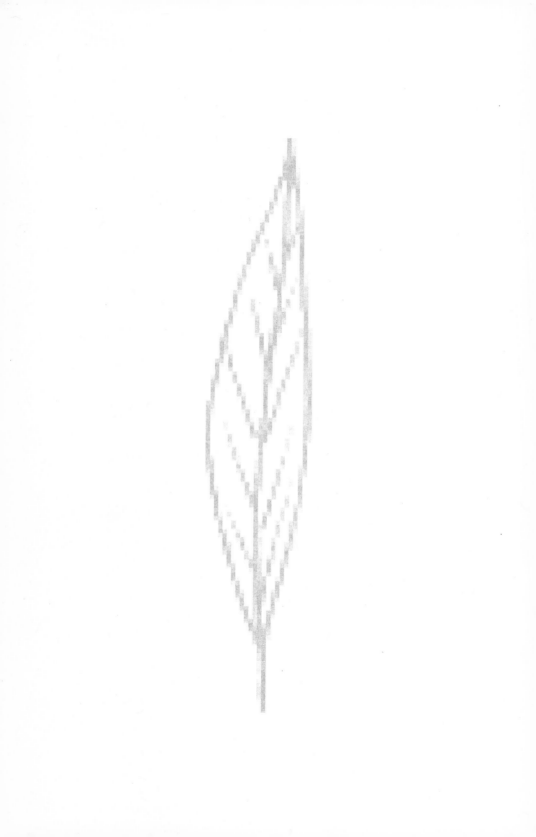

Recommended Reading / Bibliography

The teachers who came before me have been instrumental to my path. I wish to heartily recommend the works of the following authors …

Abraham-Hicks, <u>Ask and It Is Given</u>, Hay House Inc., USA, 2004

Andreas, Connirae and Tamara, <u>Core Transformation</u>, Real People Press, USA, 1994

Banis, Reimar, <u>Psychsomatic Energetics</u>, Chrystyne Jackson Enterprises, Inc., USA, 2005

Eker, T. Harv, <u>Secrets of the Millionaire Mind</u>, Harper, USA, 2005

Emoto, Masaru, <u>The Hidden Messages in Water</u>, Beyond Words Publishing, Inc., USA, 2004

Fuller, R. Buckminster, <u>Critical Path</u>, St. Martin's Press, USA, 1980

Gerber, Michael, <u>The E-Myth</u>, Harper, USA, 1995

Hawkins, David R., <u>Power versus Force</u>, Hay House Inc., USA, 2002

Hill, Napoleon, <u>Think And Grow Rich</u>, Fawcett Crest, USA, 1937

Losier, Michael, <u>Law of Attraction</u>, Michael J. Losier Enterprises, Inc., CANADA, 2006

Maday, Michael, <u>New Thought for a New Millennium</u>, Unity Books, USA, 1998

Millman, Dan, <u>Way of the Peaceful Warrior</u>, HJ Kramer Inc., USA, 1980

Moore, Robert and Gillette, Douglas, <u>King, Warrior, Magician, Lover</u>, Harper Collins, USA, 1990

Nhat-Hahn, Thich, <u>Present Moment, Wonderful Moment</u>, Parallax Press, USA, 1987

Price, John Randolph, <u>The Abundance Book</u>, Hay House Inc., USA, 1987

Ruiz, Don Miguel, <u>The Four Agreements</u>, Amber-Allen, USA, 1997

Wilde, Stuart, <u>Silent Power</u>, Hay House Inc., USA, 1997

… To name a few …

About the Author

Ariole Kesari Alei is a Trainer, Keynote Speaker, Retreat Facilitator, Relationship, Wellness, and Spirituality Coach, Energy Healer, and Yoga and Meditation Teacher.

She is the Co-Founder, with her husband Colin Hillstrom, of *Veraxis* Coaching and Training™ and HeartSong Life & Relationship Training™ including "The World's First Holistic Matchmaking Service" for personal-growth-oriented people.

Ariole has Co-Founded two non-profit societies and was the Co-Founder of *ViA* Vision Into Action Consultants.

As a Global Visionary she has met personally with His Holiness the Dalai Lama and other world leaders to discuss her visions of "A New Model of Exemplary Global Leadership".

Ariole is a former Dancer, Choreographer and Designer (see www.sharonwehnerdance.com – named after her birth name).

For information on her other writings including <u>Birds' Eye View – A Travel Guide to the Universe</u> and the trilogy <u>Awakening Instinct - the true feminine principle</u> ♥ <u>Running the Gauntlet – navigating our way to our fully embodied potential</u> ♥ <u>Windows Through Time - a 'possible evolution' story</u> as well as <u>HeartSong: Conversations About Love, Joy and Sex</u> – *Discovering the Secret to a Fulfilling Love Relationship* co-authored with her husband Colin Hillstrom ... and for advance notices of forthcoming titles ... write <u>info@veraxis.net</u>, Subject: Writings.

For information on her Keynote Speaking, Seminars, Workshops, Classes and Retreats ... including possible dates in your area ... write <u>info@veraxis.net</u>, Subject: Teachings.

To schedule an in-person or telephone Coaching or Healing Session ... write <u>info@veraxis.net</u>, Subject: Coaching/Healing or call 604-731-1783.

For information about **HeartSong Life & Relationship Training**™ write <u>info@veraxis.net</u>, Subject: HeartSong.

Inquire about our Monthly Special Offers!

HeartSong Solutions™
PO Box 647 - 2768 West Broadway
Vancouver, BC, Canada, V6K 4P4
Please visit our websites at <u>www.veraxis.net</u> and <u>www.HeartSongSolutions.ca</u>

Thank You ♡